THE PALACE MUSEUM

Compiled by the Palace Museum

Published by the Forbidden City Publishing House

The Palace Museum

Compiled by the Palace Museum

Planned by Chen Lianying, Zhang Nan and Jiang Ying

Written by Luo Wenhua and Li Min

Translated by Li Shaoyi, Zhang Yan and Yang Fan

Designed by Wang Konggang

Executive Editor: Jiang Ying

Photo: Lin Jing, Zhang Nan

Printing Manager: Ma Jingbo

Edited and published by Forbidden City Publishing House

Edited and printed for the first time in April 2006

ISBN 7-80047-546-8/J·250

Price: ￥40.00

From the Editor

Established on the basis of the Imperial Palace of the Ming and Qing dynasties, the Palace Museum is a symbol of oriental culture. One cannot be counted as having visited China if he or she has never visited the Palace Museum. This pamphlet is a token of regards from the Museum to its visitors. With its help, one could find out what important buildings he or she could visit in the Museum, what functions the buildings have, what kind of events once took place in those buildings, which figures went to and forth on the historical stages, which visiting route is the most suitable, etc.

It takes at least four hours for one to complete the visit. This pamphlet also introduces the facilities of the Museum and other details, e.g. the locations of restaurants, restrooms and souvenir shops in the Museum, the different prices of admission tickets in different periods of a year, which scenic spots one could visit after touring the Palace Museum and which transport facilities are the most convenient. This pamphlet takes into consideration the problems and difficulties a visitor might meet, so as to ensure an efficient visit. It also provides the basic information about the areas that are not open to the public in the Museum, so as to give the reader a sense of satisfaction about being acquainted with the whole Palace.

This pamphlet is elaborately composed for the convenience of your visit. At its very beginning is a general introduction of the Forbidden City, another name for the Imperial Palace. Next, it divides the open areas of the Palace Museum, according to practical visiting experience, into the Middle Route (the Three Front Halls, the Three Rear Palaces and the Imperial Garden), West Route (the Six Western Palaces), East Route (the Six Eastern Palaces) and Outer East Route (the Complex of Tranquility and Longevity and the Qianlong Garden) and marks them with different colors. The introduction of each route consists of basic information, map, main buildings, historical background, key objects, architectural features, etc. Besides, the pamphlet is armed with simple and convenient maps of various areas. When one arrives at a large or an important area, the colored map would inform one of his or her whereabouts and the names of the surrounding palaces, gates and corridors. After checking the plaque of a hall or a gate, one could visit the Imperial Palace at ease.

Try the pamphlet and enjoy yourself.

The Palace Museum

Special Notes

Access

The Palace Museum is located in the center of Beijing, north to the Street of Everlasting Peace and south to the Front Street of Prospect Hill. The bus stops of Tian'anmen Square and the Palace Museum are very near to the South and North Gates of the Museum, the only two gates open to the public. One could also come to the Museum via subway or taxi. The nearest subway stations are East of Tian'anmen and West of Tian'anmen. The taxi generally charges RMB ¥ 10 within 4 kilometers and RMB ¥ 1.6 every another kilometer.

Opening Hours

The Palace Museum opens at 8:30. From 16 April to 15 October, it stops selling tickets at 16:00 and closes at 17:00. From 16 October to 15 April, it stops selling tickets at 15:30 and closes at 16:30.

Tickets

From 1 April to 31 October, an admission ticket costs RMB ¥ 60. From 1 November to 31 March, an admission ticket costs RMB ¥ 40. The Gallery of Treasures and the Gallery of Clocks and Watches charge extra fees. The ticket for entering each gallery costs RMB ¥ 10.

Best Visiting Routes

There are two main routes to visit the Palace Museum:

(1) From south to north, i.e. the Gate of Heavenly Peace, the Gate of Origination, the Meridian Gate (the South Gate), the Three Front Halls, the Complex of Tranquility and Longevity, the Three Rear Palaces, the Six Eastern Palaces and the Six Western Palaces, the Imperial Garden, the Gate of Spiritual Valor (the North Gate).

(2) From north to south, i.e. the Gate of Spiritual Valor (the North Gate), the Imperial Garden, the Three Rear Palaces, the Six Eastern Palaces and the Six Western Palaces, the Complex of Tranquility and Longevity, the Three Front Halls, the Gate of Supreme Harmony, the Meridian Gate (the South Gate), the Gate of Heavenly Peace.

Services

■ Bag Check

To make your visit more convenient, you may check your bag free of charge at the South or North Gate of the Museum and get it back at either the South or North Gate according to your need.

■ Public Umbrella

As soon as you enter the Palace Museum, you may get a yellow umbrella for sun shading or rain sheltering. When you leave the Museum, our staff will retrieve it.

■ Guide

At the South and North Gates, one may find tour guides and audio tour, which is recorded in over ten languages and whose rent is RMB ¥ 10.

■ **Restroom**

Free four-star restrooms with air-conditioned lounges are available at the west side of the Meridian Gate, south side of the Gate of Prospering Fortune, both sides of the Gate of Heavenly Purity and the Imperial Garden as well as the north side of the East Alley.

■ **Broadcasting Station**

If you visit the Museum together with your friends but get lost, you could try to find your friends with the help of the broadcasting station located at the east side of the square before the Gate of Heavenly Purity. Its telephone number is 85117245.

■ **Post Office**

If you would like to post your belongings or postcards back home, please come to the post office in the courtyard behind the Palace of Earthly Tranquility.

■ **Police Substation**

If you run up against difficulty or emergency, please call 85117555 or 85117557. Police will help you.

■ **Visitor Center**

If you do have any questions about the Museum, please come to the visitor center in the Arrow Pavilion. Its telephone number is 85117243.

■ **First-Aid Station**

If you do not feel very well, please come to the first-aid station located near the Gate of Chastity and Obedience. Its telephone number is 85117425.

The Palace Museum

The Palace Museum

General Introduction of the Forbidden City

Plan of the Forbidden City

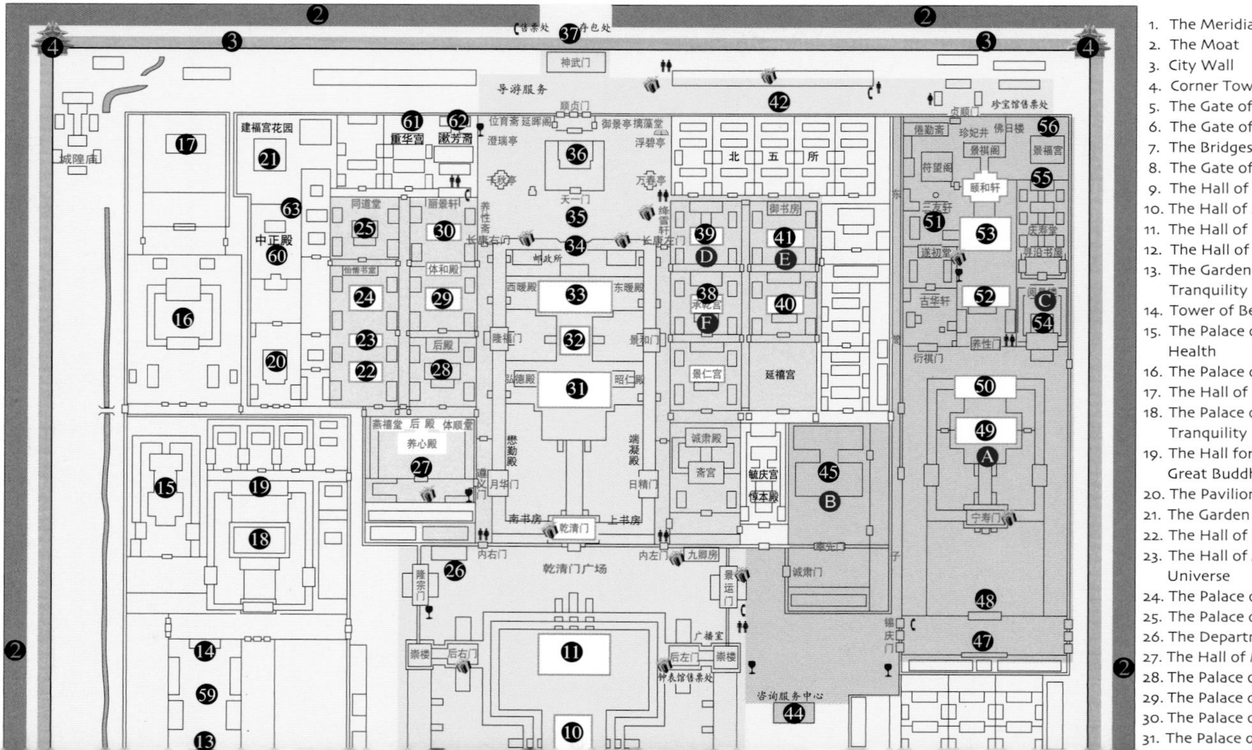

1. The Meridian Gate
2. The Moat
3. City Wall
4. Corner Tower
5. The Gate of Western Flower
6. The Gate of Eastern Flower
7. The Bridges of Golden Water
8. The Gate of Supreme Harmony
9. The Hall of Supreme Harmony
10. The Hall of Middle Harmony
11. The Hall of Preserving Harmony
12. The Hall of Military Glory
13. The Garden of Benevolent Tranquility
14. Tower of Benevolent Protection
15. The Palace of Longevity and Good Health
16. The Palace of Longevity and Peace
17. The Hall of Eminent Flowers
18. The Palace of Benevolent Tranquility
19. The Hall for Worshipping the Great Buddha
20. The Pavilion of Rain of Flowers
21. The Garden of Creating Happiness
22. The Hall of Ultimate Supremacy
23. The Hall of All-Encompassing Universe
24. The Palace of Everlasting Spring
25. The Palace of Universal Happiness
26. The Department of Military Affairs
27. The Hall of Mental Cultivation
28. The Palace of Eternal Longevity
29. The Palace of Assisting the Earth
30. The Palace of Concentrated Beauty
31. The Palace of Heavenly Purity

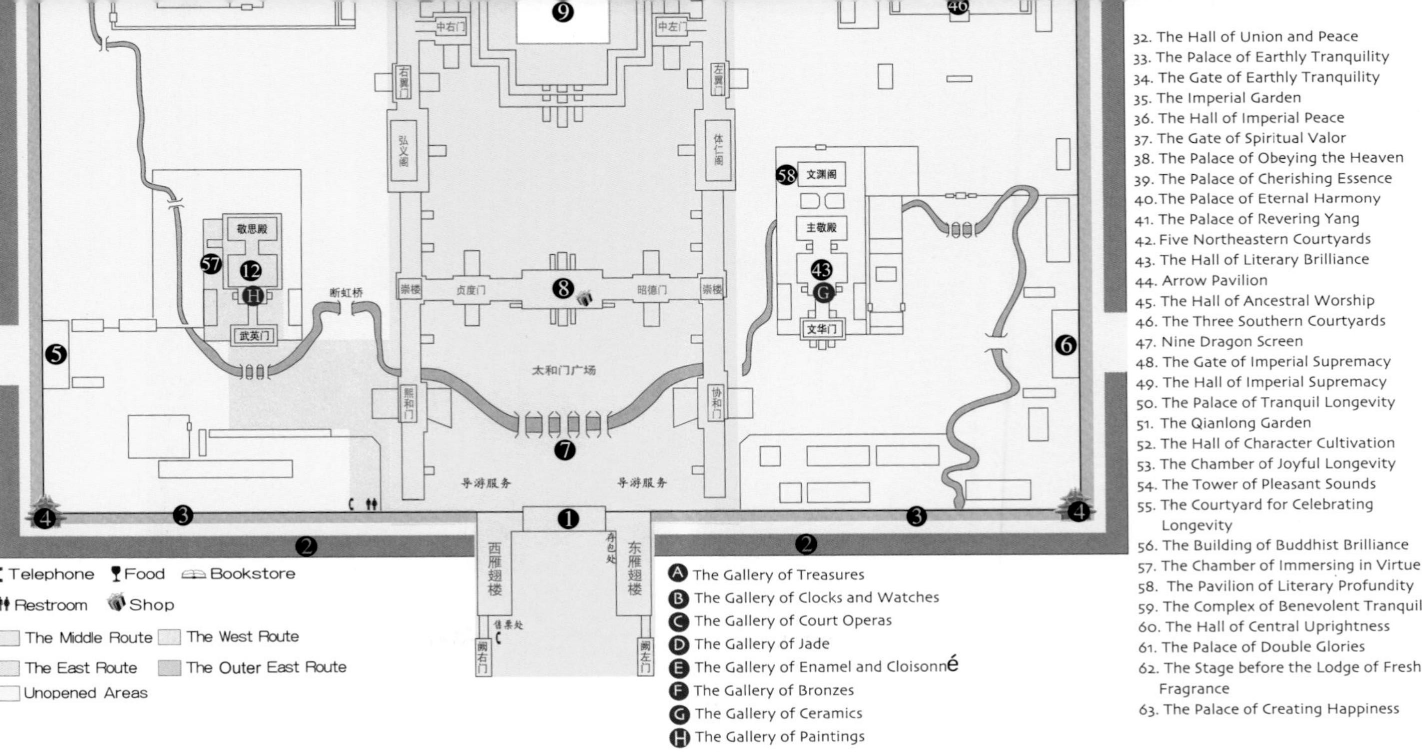
中右门
中左门
右翼门
左翼门
弘义阁
体仁阁
敬思殿
武英门
断虹桥
崇楼
贞度门
昭德门
崇楼
文渊阁
主敬殿
文华门
太和门广场
熙和门
协和门
导游服务
导游服务
西雁翅楼
东雁翅楼
存包处
售票处
阙右门
阙左门
Telephone
Food
Bookstore
Restroom
Shop
The Middle Route
The West Route
The East Route
The Outer East Route
Unopened Areas
A The Gallery of Treasures
B The Gallery of Clocks and Watches
C The Gallery of Court Operas
D The Gallery of Jade
E The Gallery of Enamel and Cloisonné
F The Gallery of Bronzes
G The Gallery of Ceramics
H The Gallery of Paintings
32. The Hall of Union and Peace
33. The Palace of Earthly Tranquility
34. The Gate of Earthly Tranquility
35. The Imperial Garden
36. The Hall of Imperial Peace
37. The Gate of Spiritual Valor
38. The Palace of Obeying the Heaven
39. The Palace of Cherishing Essence
40. The Palace of Eternal Harmony
41. The Palace of Revering Yang
42. Five Northeastern Courtyards
43. The Hall of Literary Brilliance
44. Arrow Pavilion
45. The Hall of Ancestral Worship
46. The Three Southern Courtyards
47. Nine Dragon Screen
48. The Gate of Imperial Supremacy
49. The Hall of Imperial Supremacy
50. The Palace of Tranquil Longevity
51. The Qianlong Garden
52. The Hall of Character Cultivation
53. The Chamber of Joyful Longevity
54. The Tower of Pleasant Sounds
55. The Courtyard for Celebrating Longevity
56. The Building of Buddhist Brilliance
57. The Chamber of Immersing in Virtue
58. The Pavilion of Literary Profundity
59. The Complex of Benevolent Tranquility
60. The Hall of Central Uprightness
61. The Palace of Double Glories
62. The Stage before the Lodge of Fresh Fragrance
63. The Palace of Creating Happiness

故宫

院

Zhu Di, the Yongle emperor of the Ming dynasty, is the first master of the Forbidden City.

Based on the Imperial Palace of the Ming and Qing dynasties and its collections, the Palace Museum is a comprehensive museum and, owing to its splendid architecture and rich collections, was listed as World Cultural Heritage Site in 1987. Many imperial palaces once appeared in world history. But only a few are extant today. The Imperial Palace in Beijing is one of them and attracts about 8 million visitors every year. The Chinese history epitomized in the Palace occupies an important position in cultural exchanges between China and the world.

The Imperial Palace is also known as the Forbidden City. Its construction was prepared since 1406 and completed in 1420. The period was in the reign of the third Ming emperor Yongle, whose name is Zhu Di. After the downfall of the Ming, the Palace remained to be the imperial residence of the Qing dynasty until 1924, when the last emperor Puyi was forced to leave the

Palace 12 years after his abdication. From the completion of its construction in 1420 to the downfall of the Qing dynasty in 1911, altogether 24 emperors lived and ruled there. During these 491 years, the Imperial Palace had been strictly forbidden to the general public, in whose hearts it was very sacred and mysterious. The name of the Forbidden City is closely related to traditional Chinese culture. The Chinese believed their emperor was the Son of Heaven. During their observation of the night sky, they found all the stars surrounded the Pole Star and believed the Lord of Heaven lived there and called the area around the Star "Purple Forbidden Enclosure". Accordingly, the Imperial Palace was regarded as the center of the empire and called "Purple Forbidden City" and abbreviated as the Forbidden City.

The construction of the Forbidden City was a huge project, which accumulated nationwide human, material and financial resources and lasted for 14 years. In the fourth year of the Yongle reign (1406), Zhu Di ordered to build an imperial palace in his former feudatory Beijing. Marquis Taining Chen Gui and Vice Minister of the Board of Works Wu Zhong, as officials in charge of this project, recruited artisans and civilian workers to make bricks,

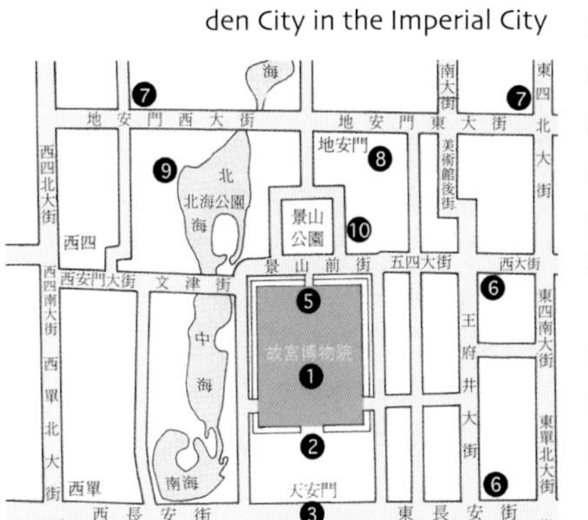

the Location of the Forbidden City in the Imperial City

1. Meridian Gate
2. Square of Meridian Gate
3. Gate of Heavenly Peace
4. Street of Everlasting Peace
5. Forbidden City
6. Wangfujing Street
7. Street Behind Gate of Earthly Peace
8. Gate of Earthly Peace
9. North Lake
10. Prospect Hill

Puyi, The last emperor of the Qing dynasty, was forced to leave the Forbidden City from the Gate of Spiritual Valor.

fire tiles, cut timber and quarry stone. It took 10 years to prepare the building materials. After four-year large-scale construction, the Forbidden City was finally built in the 18th year of the Yongle reign (1420). The next year, Zhu Di had the Ming capital moved from Nanjing to Beijing.

The Forbidden City is condensed with traditional Chinese architectural concepts and philosophical thoughts. Its strict layout, hierarchical buildings and at the same time flexible combinations perfectly reflect the essence and achievement of oriental civilization. It was built on the basis of the imperial palace of the Yuan dynasty and according to the plan of "Ancestral Temple on the left and Altar to the Gods of Earth and Grain on the right, court in the front and market at the back" recorded in *The Zhou Rites*. Its central axis coincided with the 8-kilometer-long axis of the Beijing city, on which are located the "Five Main Gates (the Gate of the Great Ming, the Gate of Heavenly Peace, the Gate of Origination, the Meridian Gate and the Gate of Supreme Harmony) and Three Main Halls (the Hall of Supreme Harmony, the Hall of Middle Harmony and the Hall of Preserving Harmony)". The Forbidden City covers 780,000 square meters while its buildings cover nearly 160,000 square meters. Surrounded with a 3, 428-meter-long city wall, it consists of 980 buildings and 8,728

The Louvre in Paris as an imperial palace was built in 1541. During the next over 200 years, it experienced four expansions and became the political and cultural center of Europe. Its space is one fourth of the Forbidden City.

The Hermitage in St. Petersburg was built in 1764. After a great fire in 1837, it was rebuilt and expanded into a luxurious palace covering an area of 17,800 square meters.

The Kremlin in Moscow accounted for one fourth of the Moscow city and was the largest imperial palace in Europe. Its space is less than one half of the Forbidden City.

The Buckingham Palace in London is the residence of the monarch of the United Kingdom. It was built in 1703 by the Duke of Buckingham and expanded by George IV in 1825. In 1837, Queen Victoria moved there. Its space is about one tenth of the Forbidden City. The throne room of the Buckingham Palace is about 600 square meters while the Hall of Supreme Harmony covers 2,377 square meters.

The imperial palace in Tokyo was rebuilt in 1888 after a fire. It covers over 217,000 square meters, about one third of the Forbidden City.

bays (a bay in China is the space among four pillars). The buildings are arranged symmetrically on both sides of the central axis, which is also the imperial route reserved for the emperor and reflects the thought "imperial authority is supreme".

The Forbidden City is mainly composed of the Outer Court and Inner Court. The former is a ceremonial quarter and centered on the Three Front Halls, i.e., the Hall of Supreme Harmony, the Hall of Middle Harmony and the Hall of Preserving Harmony, and flanked with the Hall of Literary Brilliance and the Hall of Military Glory, the places for Confucian classics explanation and imperial books printing. The latter is the residences for the emperor and empress and centered on the Three Rear Palaces, i.e., the Palace of Heavenly Purity, the Hall of Union and Peace and the Palace of Earthly Tranquility, and flanked with the Six Eastern Palaces and Six Western Palaces, residences for imperial concubines.

Most of the buildings in the Forbidden City belong to wood-structured architecture traditional in China, which makes strict demands on the quality and quantity of timber. Timber cutting was a dangerous work. The cut timbers would be tied into rafts, which would be flushed into rivers by floods and travel three or four years to Beijing via the Yangtze River and the Grand Canal. Bricks and tiles were also in great demand. It took over 80 million bricks to build the Forbidden City. The total weight of the bricks amounted to 1,930,000 tons.

With long and bright history, unique and majestic architecture as well as rich and precious collections, the Forbidden City is one of the most famous imperial palaces in the world. In 1961, it was listed as a key historical and cultural site under state protection by the State Council, the People's Republic of China. In

1987, it was listed as World Cultural Heritage by UNESCO. The former Imperial Palace is now a world-renowned historical and artistic museum and a popular scenic spot.

Origins of building materials and transportation routes

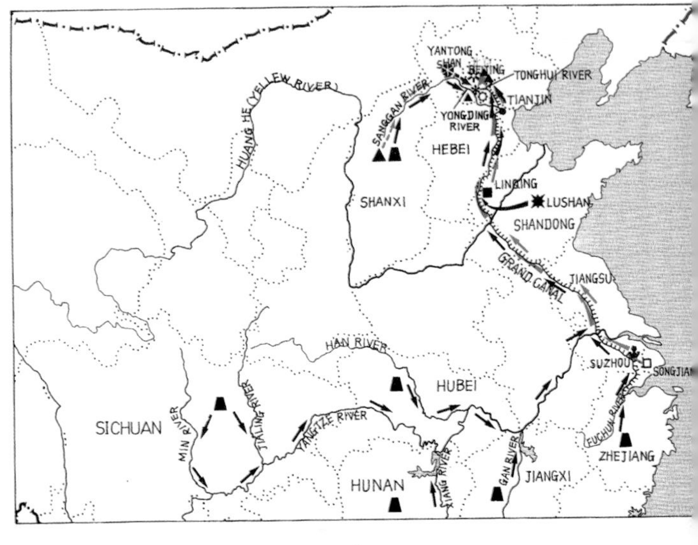

KEY TO MAP

- timber
- timber transportation route
- *cheng jiang zhuan* 'settled clay bricks'
- *jin zhuan*' golden bricks'
- stone: different varieties, vicinity of Beijing
- lime
- lime transportation route
- red clay
- red clay transportation route
- gold clay
- gold clay transportation route
- gold (leaf etc.)
- gold transportation route
- black roof tiles (Beijing)
- glazed tiles and ornaments (Beijing)

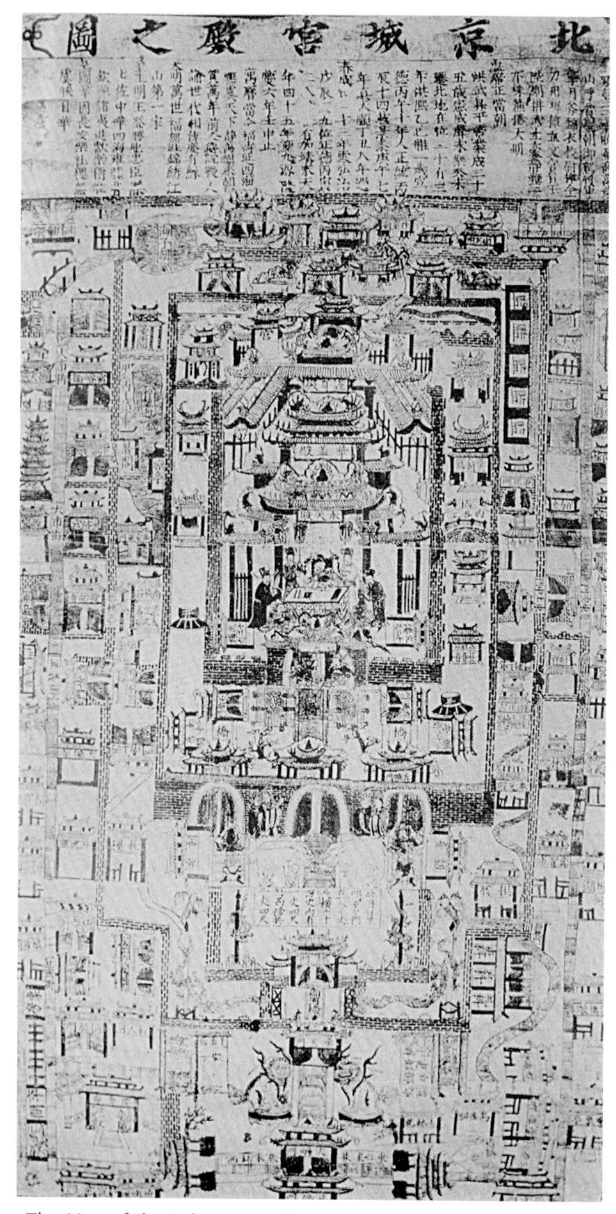

The Map of the Palaces in Beijing Drawn in the 15th Century

The Gates, Wall and Surrounding Water of The Forbidden City

The National Gate in the Ming and Qing dynasties, no longer extant today

The Forbidden City is 3.5 kilometers long in circumference. The trapezoid-shaped city wall is pierced with four gates: the Meridian Gate, the Gate of Spiritual Valor, the Gate of Eastern Flower and the Gate of Western Flower, guarded with four exquisite corner towers and surrounded by a 52-meter-wide moat. At sunrise and sunset, the corner tower and the moat set off each other and form a charming view.

With the Forbidden City as its center, Beijing in the Ming and

Buildings along the Central Axis of the Imperial City

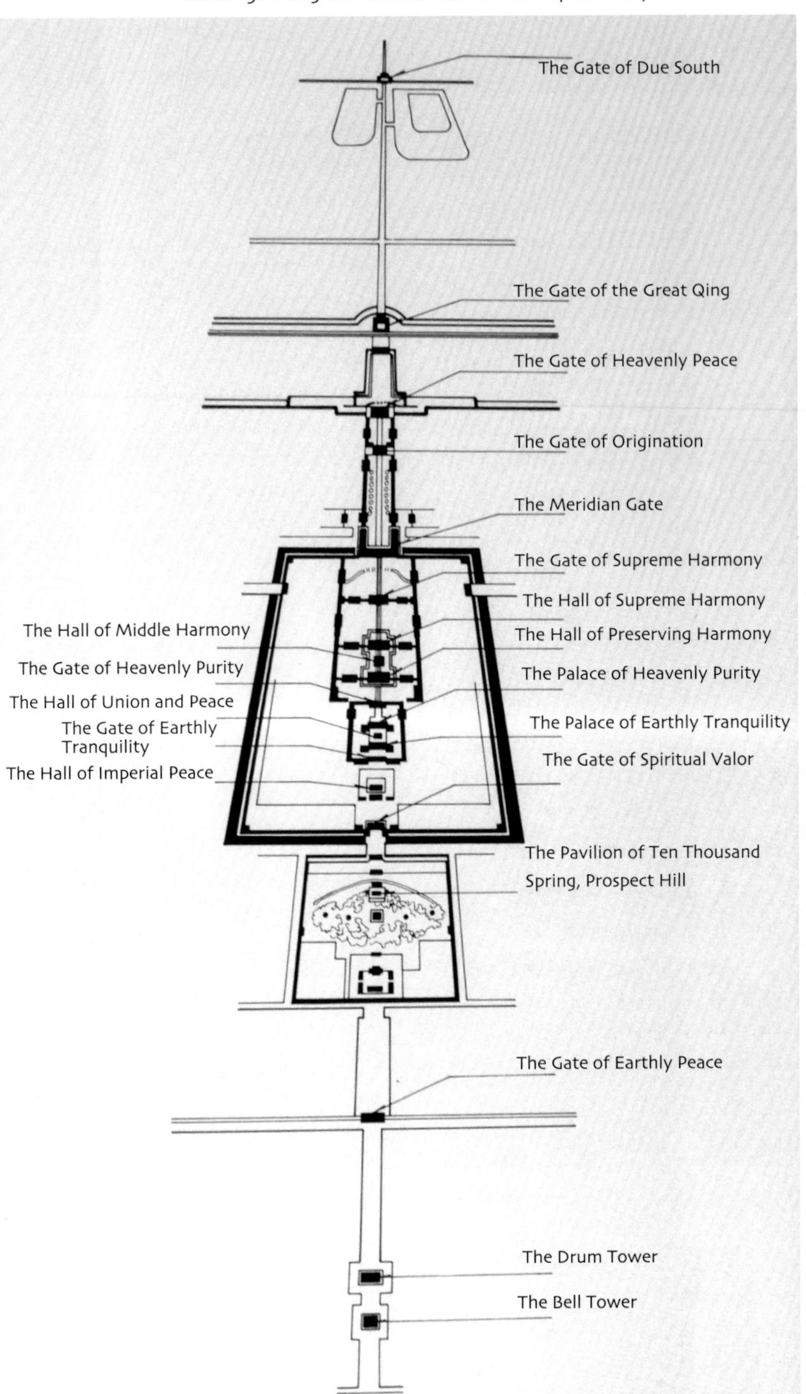

Qing dynasties consists of four cities, one surrounded with another. They are the Forbidden City, Imperial City, Inner City and Outer City. Their main gates are located on the central axis of Beijing, which is the imperial route paved with huge flagstones that could be seen as soon as one enters the Palace Museum.

In the Qianlong period of the Qing dynasty (1736-1795), a mad monk once succeeded in entering the Gate of Eastern Flower with the help of a knife and the guards failed to block his way. After this incident, all the guards on duty were punished severely.

The Meridian Gate symbolizing imperial majesty looked quite desolate at the end of the Qing dynasty.

A corner of the Meridian Gate with wild goose wings

The Meridian Gate: the Gate With Five Phoenixes

The Meridian Gate is the front gate of the Imperial Palace. Its name has something to do with *fengshui*: the Gate is located in the south of the Palace and the south corresponds to the Earthly Branch Wu (meridian), hence the name Meridian Gate.

The majestic gate consists of a high rostrum with two symmetrical wings that could hide warriors and might have defensive function, four square pavilions on both ends of the wings and a main tower. Its total height is nearly 38 meters. With one tower in the center and four pavilions on the flanks, the Gate looks like a big bird about to fly, so it is also known as the Gate with Wild Goose Wings and the Gate with Five Phoenixes.

The Gate has five passages that had strict hierarchical stipulations. The central passage was reserved for the emperor. But four other persons were allowed to use the passage once in their lives. The first was the empress. On the wedding day, the empress would enter the Palace from the central passage of the Meridian Gate on a sedan chair. The other three were the top three winners of the Palace Examination, the highest-level examination in ancient China. This special honor was to show the emperor's attention and favor towards literati.

Bell and drum were placed on the wings of the Gate. When the emperor went to the Temple of Heaven and the Temple of Earth, bell would be struck. When he went to the Ancestral Temple, drum would be beaten. When a grand ceremony was held, the bell and drum would be struck and beaten at the same time.

The square before the Gate covers 9,900 square meters. It was the very place to hold important ceremonies and bestow officials with imperial favors. In traditional festivals, seasonal food would be granted to officials there while the subjects were welcome to come there to admire beautiful lanterns, so as to show that the imperial family enjoyed being together with the people and the whole nation joined in the jubilation.

Now the Gate is used as an exhibition gallery for the visitors to admire exquisite objects as well as look down at the square and feel the sense of being an emperor.

Beheading outside the Meridian Gate is merely hearsay. But court flogging did exist in the Ming dynasty, when the disobedient officials would be taken to the square before the Meridian Gate, flogged and sometimes beaten to death by Embroidered-Uniform Guards.

The Gate of Spiritual Valor bearing the heavy history of the Forbidden City

The Gate of Spiritual Valor

As a smaller counterpart of the Meridian Gate, the Gate of Spiritual Valor is the north gate of the Imperial Palace. Its original name was Xuanwu (the North). As the name of Emperor Kangxi (r. 1662-1722) was Xuanye, the Gate was renamed Shenwu (spiritual valor) to avoid the taboo. Bell and drum were placed in the five-bay tower on the Gate and were struck and beaten at night by ceremonial guards. When the emperor was not in the Imperial Palace, the bell would be struck 108 times at 7 p.m. Every two hours, drum would be beaten. In the early morning, bell would be struck again. When the emperor lived in the Imperial Palace, the guards would only beat the drum every two hours. The Gate of Spiritual Valor was the usual entrance and exit for imperial consorts and imperial family members. In 1644, the last Ming emperor Chongzhen (r. 1628-1644) hurried through the Gate, came to the foot of the Prospect Hill and hanged himself on a tree after the peasant insurgents entered Beijing.

In the beginning years of the Shunzhi reign (1644-1661), Empress Dowager Xiaozhuang issued a decree to stipulate that those who dared to introduce girls that had bound their feet into the Imperial Palace would be punished with decapitation. This decree was hung inside the Gate of Spiritual Valor. When the Qing emperor came back to the Imperial Palace from the Mountain Retreat or Summer Palace, he usually entered the Imperial Palace from the Gate of Spiritual Valor, which was also the gate often used by the imperial consorts and imperial family members. When the emperor went out of the Imperial Palace for a tour, he would exit from the Meridian Gate. But his consorts had to go out of the Imperial Palace from the Gate of Spiritual Valor. If the emperor accompanied empress dowager for a tour, they would go out of the Imperial Palace from the Gate of Spiritual Valor together.

Ramp for horses at the Gate of Eastern Flower

The Gate of Eastern Flower

The Gate of Eastern Flower and the Gate of Western Flower are symmetrical and located respectively in the southeast and southwest of the Forbidden City. As they served as entrances for officials, if they were located in due east and west, they would be too near to the Inner Court and that would be offensive to the imperial family. Outside the Gate of Eastern Flower, there is a Horse-Dismounting Stele, at which the officials had to dismount from their horsebacks, in order to show their reverence for the Imperial Palace.

The pass of the Qing official

When the officials went to court, they would dismount from their horsebacks at the Stele and then enter the Imperial Palace on foot. Those whom the emperor granted the permission to ride horses or take carriages in the Imperial Palace were exceptions. After the Qing emperors died, their coffins would be carried out of the Imperial Palace from the Gate of Eastern Flower and sent to the Hall of Longevity of the Emperor in the Prospect Hill. At the Festival of the Dead Spirits, the imperial family would have dharma boats burned outside the Gate. In the tower above the Gate were stored the emperor's parade armors, which would be aired once a year.

The Horse-Dismounting Stele outside the Gate of Eastern Flower. The officials should dismount from their horsebacks there and enter the Palace on foot.

Old photo of the Gate of Western Flower

The Gate of Western Flower

The Gate of Western Flower had similar function to the Gate of Eastern Flower. When the emperor and empress dowager visited imperial gardens, they would go out of the Imperial Palace from the Gate because the imperial gardens like West Garden and the Summer Palace are located on the west of the Forbidden City.

In the 18th year of the Jiaqing reign (1813), when the believers of the Heavenly Order Religion attacked the Imperial Palace, they entered the Palace from the Gate of Western Flowers.

In the 7th year of the Guangxu reign (1881), the coffin of Empress Dowager Ci'an went out of the Imperial Palace from the Gate of Western Flower out of mysterious reason. The 11-year-old Guangxu emperor knelt beside the paved path outside the Gate, bidding farewell with tears to the benevolent and understanding Empress Dowager in his heart. He was brought into the Imperial Palace by his aunt Empress Dowager Cixi when he was four year old and since then had been living on tenterhooks under the tight control of his aunt. Only the kind Empress Dowager Ci'an often encouraged and supported him, so that he could feel a trace of warmth in the Imperial Palace.

City Wall and Corner Tower

The city wall of the Imperial Palace was traditional Chinese city-defending installation. It is 9.9 meters high, 8.62 meters wide at the bottom and 6.66 meters wide at the top, on which five or six horses could gallop abreast. Every 20 meters under the wall is a drain mouth. The wall is tamped with tight earth and covered with over 12 million fine-quality bricks fired in Linqing, Shandong, each of which is 48 centimeters long, 24 centimeters wide, 12 centimeters thick and 24 kilograms heavy.

The corner tower is a charming view of the Forbidden City. With ingenious design and exquisite structure, it may be rated as a miracle in the architectural history of China.

Corner tower witnessing the vicissitudes of the history of the Forbidden City

Exquisite and splendid Corner Tower as a classic work of ancient Chinese architecture

Southeastern Corner Tower in 1922

Outer Golden Water River

It is said that after Zhu Di seized the throne from his nephew, he was distracted all the time. One night, an immortal said to him in his dream: "if you want to keep the throne, you have to build a tower with 9 beams, 18 pillars and 72 ridges to stabilize the Palace." Zhu Di hastily asked how to build it. The immortal smiled and kept silent. The Emperor became so anxious that he awoke. As a result, he ordered his Board of Works to build a tower with 9 beams, 18 pillars and 72 ridges at each corner of the Imperial Palace, so that his Palace could be stable and carried forward by his posterity. The artisans racked their brains and finally got inspired by cricket cage and succeeded in building the towers.

Moat

The Forbidden City is surrounded with a 52-meter-wide and 6-meter-deep moat, whose steep banks are paved with slabs. The water originated from the Hill of Jade Spring in the western suburbs of Beijing, passed the Summer Palace, Back Lake, the west gate of Prospect Hill, and finally merged into the moat. According to the Qing documents, the moat was planted with lotus from the Kangxi reign (1662-1722). The lotus seeds and fruits would be consumed in the Palace as well as sold in the markets. After the Jiaqing reign (1796-1820), the moat was rented to lotus growers. These facts show that even the imperial family was meticulous in the planning of revenue and expenditure.

The moat with lotus blossoms

Golden Water River

There are two golden water rivers in Beijing. One is called Inner Golden Water River, located at the back of the Meridian Gate; the other is known as Outer Golden Water River, located before the Gate of Heavenly Peace. The former meanders over 2,000 meters in the Imperial Palace and is spanned with 21 bridges and over 10 culverts. Its practical functions include draining rain, providing water source and extinguishing fire. Besides, it is an indispensable element for beautifying the Forbidden City and humidifying the air.

Inner Golden Water River surrounding and protecting the Meridian Gate

The Middle Route

The Map of the Middle Route

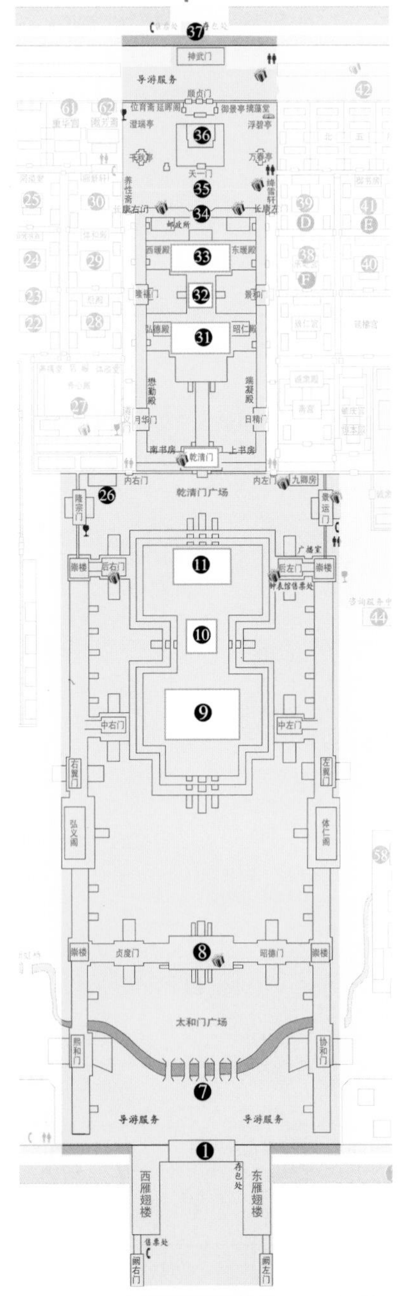

1. The Meridian Gate
7. The Bridges of Golden Water
8. The Gate of Supreme Harmony
9. The Hall of Supreme Harmony
10. The Hall of Middle Harmony
11. The Hall of Preserving Harmony
26. The Department of Military Affairs
31. The Palace of Heavenly Purity
32. The Hall of Union and Peace
33. The Palace of Earthly Tranquility
34. The Gate of Earthly Tranquility
35. The Imperial Garden
36. The Hall of Imperial Peace
37. The Gate of Spiritual Valor

The Middle Route covers the most important areas in the Outer and Inner Courts, including, from south to north, the Square before the Gate of Supreme Harmony, the Gate of Supreme Harmony, the Three Front Halls, the Square before the Gate of Heavenly Purity, the Three Rear Palaces, Imperial Garden and the Hall of Imperial Peace.

The Inner Golden Water Bridges in the Square before the Gate of Supreme Harmony display the strict hierarchical institution.

The Square before The Gate of Supreme Harmony

The Inner Golden Water River passes the Square before the Gate of Supreme Harmony and is spanned with five marble bridges. In the north of the Square is the Gate of Supreme Harmony; in the east and west are the Ming and Qing government offices, e. g. Grand Secretariat, Daily Records Office and Translation Chamber that was responsible for translating Manchu and Han Chinese documents.

Inner Golden Water River

Inner Golden Water River

The jade-belt-shaped Inner Golden Water River meanders in the Square before the Gate of Supreme Harmony and enlivens the tranquil space. The spectacular five marble bridges on the River could serve as an example to reflect the hierarchical system of the feudal dynasties: the bridge in the middle was reserved for the emperor. With a length of 23.5 meters and a width of 6 meters, it is the most splendid bridge in the Forbidden City. The two bridges beside it were intended for princes and dukes. The other two were meant for high-ranking civil officials and military officers.

The Gate of Supreme Harmony

As the highest gate in the Forbidden City, the Gate of Supreme Harmony was used by the emperor to listen to the reports of his officials in the Ming dynasty. In the Qing dynasty, the place for this routine work was changed to the Gate of Heavenly Purity. After the Qing dominated the Central Plains, Emperor Shunzhi released a decree at the Gate of Imperial Supremacy (present-day Gate of Supreme Harmony) to announce general amnesty in the nation. The Gate of Supreme Harmony today was rebuilt in the 20th year of the Guangxu reign (1894). It is the youngest architecture in the Forbidden City.

The Splendid Gate of Supreme Harmony
The Ming emperor listened to the reports of his officials here in the early morning.

The pair of the Ming bronze lions before the Gate of Supreme Harmony is the largest pair in China.

The bronze lion represents the majesty of the emperor.

Before the Gate of Supreme Harmony is a pair of bronze lions cast in the Ming dynasty. The right front paw of the male lion steps on a sphere denoting imperial power while the left front paw of the lioness fondles her cub denoting flourishing posterity. The ancient Chinese believed that lion symbolized might and valor. In Buddhist doctrine, lion is the Guardian. It is said that the amount of the mane curls could tell a lion statue's status. As a result, the mane curls of the lion statues in the Imperial Palace are more than those of the lion statues in prince mansions.

Mythical animals on the ridge corner of the Hall of Supreme Harmony. The number of the mythical animals could tell the grade of an ancient building.

The Three Front Halls

Behind the Gate of Supreme Harmony is the Square before the Hall of Supreme Harmony, which covers over 30,000 square meters and is the largest square in the Forbidden City. In the north of the Square is an 8.13-meter-high marble terrace, on whose three tiers are placed altogether 18 bronze censers. When grand ceremonies were held in the Hall of Supreme Harmony, fresh pine and cypress branches would be burned in the censers. The smoke curling upwards would create a solemn and mysterious atmosphere. The furnishings on the terrace include a sundial and a standard measure denoting authority as well as a pair of bronze tortoise and crane denoting longevity.

Bronze crane

Bronze tortoise

Three-tier marble terrace

On the three-tier terrace stand three majestic halls, i.e. the Hall of Supreme Harmony, the Hall of Middle Harmony and the Hall of Preserving Harmony. The Hall of Supreme Harmony was mainly used for grand ceremonies, e.g. enthronement, wedding, expedition, celebrations of the New Year's Day, Winter Solstice and the emperor's birthday, state banquet, etc. On the occasion of a ceremony, bronze status markers would be placed on the Square for the officials to find their kowtow places. Besides, complicated insignias would also be placed on the Square, forming a magnificent sight.

Mark for an official to find his position in imperial ceremony: status mark

Incense burners on the three-tier terrace create a solemn and mysterious atmosphere for imperial ceremony.

Silver Storage of the Qing: the Hall of Expanding Justice

The Pavilion of Manifesting Benevolence and The Pavilion of Expanding Justice

The traditional aesthetic standards in China appreciate the beauty of balance and symmetry, which is fully reflected in the architecture of the Forbidden City: the Pavilion of Manifesting Benevolence and the Pavilion of Expanding Justice are located on the east and west sides of the Square before the Hall of Supreme Harmony and served as human and material resource centers of the Qing dynasty.

In the early Qing dynasty, the Pavilion of Manifesting Benevolence was used to give examinations of "Bo Xue Hong Ci" (Profound Knowledge and Flowery Language) for recommended literati while the Pavilion of Expanding Justice was the imperial storage for gold, silver and precious stones.

The Hall of Supreme Harmony

The Hall of Supreme Harmony, popularly known as the Hall of Golden Throne, is the highest-grade building in the Forbidden City and the largest hall in Chinese ancient architecture extant. As the symbol of imperial authority, the Hall is supported with 72 pillars, covered with two-eave hipped roof and decorated with gold paintings. In the center of the 2,377-square-meter Hall are the six 13-meter-high gilded pillars. The floor is paved with rare clay bricks, which, owing to their fine quality, complicated techniques and great value, are called "golden bricks". Since the 34th year of the Kangxi reign (1695) when the Hall was rebuilt, over 300 years have passed, but the bricks still look like black jade, bright and smooth.

The Plaque of the Hall of Supreme Harmony

The symbol of imperial authority: the Hall of Supreme Harmony

Caisson Ceiling of the Hall of Supreme Harmony.

The throne is set on a seven-step *nanmu* platform, which is carved with exquisite design. On both sides of the throne are furnished symmetrically with auspicious ornaments, such as cranes, incense pavilions, *luduan* (unicorns that could travel 9,000 kilometers a day and understand all the languages in the world) and elephants with vases on their backs. The center of the ceiling is decorated with an exquisite caisson, which is mainly used in high-grade imperial architecture. This is the magnificent environment for the Son of Heaven to display his supreme power.

Gilded pillars and golden tiles set off each other.

The golden throne displays the majesty of the emperor ruling over his state.

The Hall of Middle Harmony

The Hall of Middle Harmony had many functions: Before the emperor went to the Hall of Supreme Harmony to preside over grand ceremonies, he would come here first to accept felicitations of important officials. When honorary title was conferred upon empress dowager, he would come here to review the memorial drafted by officials. When the imperial pedigree was updated every ten years, he would come here to review it. One day before going to Agricultural Altar for self-plowing, he would come here to examine the farming tools. Before he offered sacrifices in the Temples and Altars, he would come here to read sacrificial writings. The Hall of Middle Harmony was also the very place to hold small-scale banquets.

The square Hall of Middle Harmony was a busy hall of state affairs.

The Hall of Preserving Harmony was the Place of Palace Examination presided over by the emperor and most yearned for by the literati in China.

The Hall of Preserving Harmony

The Hall of Preserving Harmony is also located on the three-tier terrace and is another high-grade hall in the Forbidden City. When the emperor came from the Inner Court to the Outer Court to attend grand ceremonies, he first came to the Hall of Preserving Harmony to change ceremonial robe. After that, he would go to the Hall of Middle Harmony to accept felicitations from executive officials and wait for the auspicious time to go to the Hall of Supreme Harmony to preside over the grand ceremonies.

The Hall of Preserving Harmony usually served as imperial banquet hall and examination place. In the early Qing dynasty, the Shunzhi and Kangxi emperors even lived there for a long time. In the 54th year of the Qianlong reign (1789), the Hall became the place for giving the Palace Examination, the highest-level examination in feudal China for official selection. Many high-ranking officials started their official careers here.

The names of the Three Front Halls came from *The Doctrine of the Mean,* telling that the existences of all the beings are the results of harmony. With their harmonious names, the Three Front Halls lay a solid foundation for a stable rule.

The Hall of Preserving Harmony in 1900

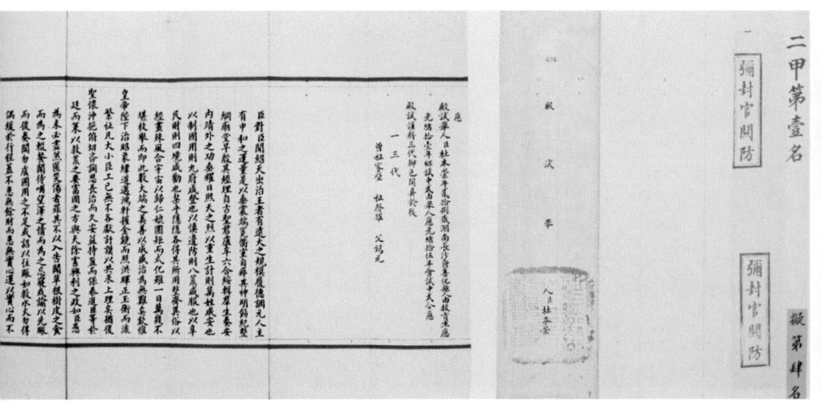

二甲第壹名

彌封官關防

彌封官關防

擬第肆名

Document indicating places in Palace Examination

The throne in the Hall of Preserving Harmony
The wide space in the Hall was perfect for Palace Examination, the highest-level examination in the Ming and Qing China.

Stone Ramp Carved with Dragons and Clouds

The largest stone carving in the Forbidden City is the ramp with dragon and cloud design behind the Hall of Preserving Harmony. It is 16.57 meters long, 3.07 meters wide, 1.7 meters thick and over 200 tons heavy.

How was this huge stone transported to the Imperial Palace? The stone came from Dashiwo, about 50 kilometers away from the Palace. It was quarried by tens of thousands of civilian workers and over 6,000 soldiers.

To transport it, wells were sunk every half a kilometer. In bitterly cold winter, water was drawn from the wells and then splashed onto the ground. After an ice road was formed, 20,000 civilian workers and over 1,000 mules spent 28 days in dragging the stone. The whole project cost 110,000 taels of silver. As two stone carvings were needed on two sides of the three-tier terrace, two huge stones were prepared. But because of the difficult transportation task, it was impossible to transport the other stone, which is still kept in Dashiwo today.

This stone carving with cloud and dragon design is the largest and most exquisite work of stone carving art in the Imperial Palace.

The dividing line between the Outer Court and Inner Court: the Square before the Gate of Heavenly Purity

The Square before the Gate of Heavenly Purity

The Square before the Gate of Heavenly Purity is the dividing line between the Outer Court in the south and the Inner Court in the north. The former was the ceremonial quarter while the latter was the residential quarter. In the eyes of the emperor, the former symbolized the State while the latter symbolized the Family. The ancient Chinese believed that the State was closely related to the Imperial Family and, no matter where, the emperor should exercise his imperial authority.

In the east and west of the Square were two forbidden gates, the Gate of Prospering Fortune and the Gate of Flourishing Posterity. All the officials who went to court would pass these gates, before which imperial guards and relevant officials would examine their qualifications.

The Department of Military Affairs, the most powerful organization in the Qing court, lay in tiny rooms.

The Department of Military Affairs

The row of low houses west to the Gate of Heavenly Purity is the Department of Military Affairs, which was established in the seventh year of the Yongzheng reign (1729) as a temporary organization to deal with emergent military affairs. Owing to its efficiency and secrecy, it was finally settled as a formal government department and even expanded into a comprehensive organ similar to the Privy Council.

Holding Court at the Gate of Heavenly Purity Morning court was a routine work for the Qing emperor. It was held at the Gate of Heavenly Purity. The emperor would sit on a throne temporarily placed in the center of the Gate and surrounded by officials responsible for recording his words and behaviors and assisting him in dealing with day-to-day affairs. At morning court, a minister would kneel down and report general affairs. Secret affairs would be reported when irrelevant officials and guards withdrew. The emperor would issue an order after each report. The ministers would deal with specific affairs according to the imperial orders.

Every day, the Military Ministers and Clerks would sit on the floor before the emperor and listen to imperial decrees. Back to the Department, the Military Clerks would write down the decrees immediately and strictly according to the original imperial version and forward them to eunuchs for imperial review. After the emperor approved, the decrees would be released.

The plaque of the Gate of Flourishing Posterity
The arrowhead left on the plaque when the peasant insurgents of the Heavenly Order Religion attacked the Imperial Palace

The Gate of Flourishing Posterity

The Gate of Flourishing Posterity was a forbidden gate. When the emperor asked his officials to come to the Palace, the servants of the officials had to stop 20 steps away from the Gate. However, when peasant insurgents of the Heavenly Order Religion broke into the Palace from the Gate of Western Flower on 15 September 1813, it was at this Gate that the insurgents fought with imperial guards and finally lost the clash, whose trace, an arrowhead, could still be found today on the plaque of the Gate.

The Gate of Flourishing Posterity

The Gate of Prospering Fortune

The Gate of Prospering Fortune and the Gate of Flourishing Posterity were perfect places to control the entrance and exit of the people who visited the Imperial Palace. When objects were taken out of the Imperial Palace, they should be examined according to relevant records at the Gate of Prospering Fortune. Most officials were not allowed to enter the Imperial Palace on horsebacks or in carriages. Even those who were allowed to do so had to dismount from their horsebacks at the Gate of Prospering Fortune.

The Three Rear Palaces

Behind the Gate of Heavenly Purity is the residential quarter of the imperial couple. A 50-meter-long and 10-meter-wide causeway connects the Gate and the Palace of Heavenly Purity. It was reserved for the emperor while the others had to make a detour via terraces on the east and west of the square before the Palace. The residential quarter of the imperial couple mainly consists of three buildings, which are surrounded with wings and located in a large courtyard. As the emperor's bedchamber was moved out of the Palace of Heavenly Purity in the Yongzheng period of the Qing dynasty, the wings were converted into various offices, storages and studies.

Panoramic View of the Inner Court.

The residential quarter of the imperial couple originally only consisted of two palaces, i.e. the Palace of Heavenly Purity and the Palace of Earthly Tranquility. In the Jiajing reign of the Ming dynasty (1522-1566), the Hall of Union and Peace, named after "the union of the heaven and earth brings peace" in *The Book of Changes*, was inserted between the two palaces.

The causeway before the Palace of Heavenly Purity displays the emperor's concept of ruling China: State was closely related to the Imperial Family.

The Palace of Heavenly Purity

As the largest building in the Inner Court, the Palace of Heavenly Purity was the residence of 16 Ming and early Qing emperors. On the terrace before the Palace are placed the same furnishings as on the terrace before the Hall of Supreme Harmony. On the east and west of the terrace is a pair of gilded pavilions symbolizing the Territory and State and emphasizing the imperial authority.

In the Palace, a plaque with the inscription of "Zhengda Guangming" (Just and Honorable) by Emperor Shunzhi is hung above the throne covered with golden lacquer and carved with dragons. The throne stands on a square platform and against a screen, which is engraved with extracts from *The Book of History* and *The Book of Changes* transcribed by Emperor Kangxi. Though the Palace of Heavenly Purity was the residence of the Ming emperors, they usually lived in the partitioned-off sections or side halls of the Palace. Most Ming emperors passed away here. Their coffins would be placed here for 27 days before moved to the Ming tombs.

Ming Cases in the Palace of Heavenly Purity In the Ming dynasty, some mysterious cases occurred in the Palace of Heavenly Purity: Emperor Taichang (r. 1620) died 40 days after enthronement. His death caused chaos in the court as he died after taking two red pills presented by protocol official Li Kezhuo. The ministers accused Li Kezhuo of poisoning the Emperor. But because of the complicated conflicts among different factions in the court, this case closed with no result. It is known as "Red Pill Case". Another case is "Moving out of the Palace". After Emperor Taichang (r. 1620) died, Concubine Li of Emperor Taichang, with the support of Concubine Zheng of Emperor Wanli (r. 1573-1620), refused to leave the Palace of Heavenly Purity and was finally forced by the ministers to move out of the Palace.

Before the peasant insurgents led by Li Zicheng broke through Beijing, the last Ming emperor Chongzhen (r. 1628-1644) tried his best to escape from Beijing but failed. He returned to the Palace of Heavenly Purity desolately. After ordering his consorts to commit suicide, killing and injuring his daughters and asking his sons to leave, he went to the Prospect Hill and hanged himself at the foot of the Hill.

Extensive Functions of the Palace of Heavenly Purity The functions of the Palace of Heavenly Purity greatly changed in the Qing dynasty. In the Shunzhi (1644-1661) and Kangxi (1662-1722) reigns, the emperor not only lived there, but also summoned his officials for consultation, received envoys, read memorials and held Inner Court ceremonies there. After the imperial bedchamber was moved to the Hall of Mental Cultivation in the Yongzheng reign (1723-1735), the Palace of Heavenly Purity became the area for handling state af-

光明
弘敷五典無輕民事惟難
惟精惟一道積于厥躬

Many secrets must be hidden in the luxurious Palace of Heavenly Purity .

fairs and accepting felicitations. However, it was ritually regarded as the formal residence of the emperor, who should come here every day to read "Holy Teachings" of former emperors. Before grand ceremonies, the emperor should leave the Inner Court from the Palace of Heavenly Purity. No matter where he died, his coffin would be placed in the Palace, so as to accord with the tradition of "ending one's longevity in the formal residence".

After being promoted or degraded and when asking for leave, the Qing officials would be summoned to the Palace of Heavenly Purity, where the emperor would release his final decision. The Palace of Heavenly Purity was also the place to receive envoys from other countries and vassal states.

The Plaque with the Inscription of "Zhengda Guangming" (Just and Honorable)

"Zhengda Guangming" (Just and Honorable) was written by Emperor Shunzhi, the first Qing emperor to rule the Forbidden City. After he died, his son Emperor Kangxi admired his calligraphy so much that Kangxi had "Zhengda Guangming" inscribed and wrote an ode to it. The plaque today was re-inscribed in January 1797 and has been hung in the Palace of Heavenly Purity for over 200 years.

This plaque became mysterious and sublime in the Yongzheng period (1723-1735), when the Yongzheng emperor established the secret institution of successor selection to prevent the

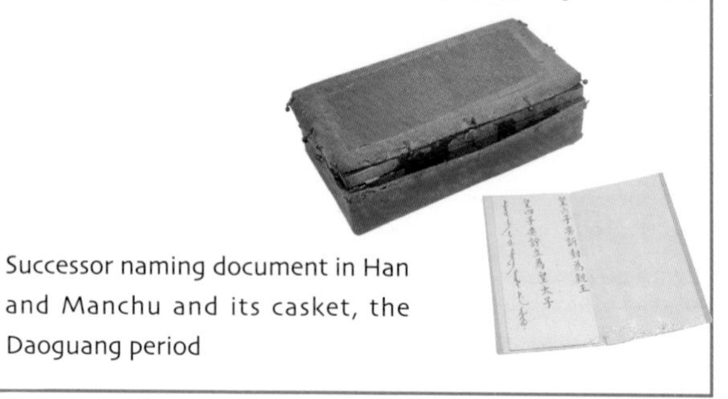

Successor naming document in Han and Manchu and its casket, the Daoguang period

princes from vying for the throne: he wrote the name of the successor on a piece of paper, had it locked in a casket and then hid the casket behind the plaque. Another copy was also prepared and carried on his person at all times. After the emperor died, the two copies would be compared. If matched, the name of the successor would be announced. This institution played an active role in stabilizing political situation and strengthening imperial power.

The Banquet of Thousand Elders To demonstrate imperial favor, the emperor gave banquets to his officials on the New Year's Day and the emperor's birthday. The tables were placed in two lines on the terrace and causeway before the Palace of Heavenly Purity. Tall tables and chairs were prepared for princes and dukes, while low tables and chairs were prepared for ministers.

In the heyday of the Qing dynasty, banquets were often given in the Palace of Heavenly Purity. In the spring of the 61st year of the Kangxi reign (1722), the 69-year-old Kangxi emperor organized a grand banquet called "the Banquet of Thousand Elders" in the Palace and invited 730 people above 60 years old in Beijing. This graceful tradition was carried forward by the Qianlong emperor, who held an even grander banquet, with over 800 tables and over 3,000 elders from various parts of China, in the fiftieth anniversary of his enthronement (1785). In January 1796, when the 85-year-old Qianlong emperor gave the banquet as super-sovereign in the Hall of Imperial Supremacy in the Complex of Tranquility and Longevity, 3,056 people (over 8,000 people in some version) attended the banquet. This event became a favorite topic at that time.

Imperial banquet with fabulous dishes

A great emperor in Chinese history: Emperor Kangxi

The Hall of Luminous Benevolence

The Palace of Heavenly Purity in the early Qing dynasty was actually an office and study. The real bedchamber was the Hall of Luminous Benevolence on the east of the Palace. Emperor Kangxi (r. 1662-1722) moved there when he was 16 years old and lived there for 53 years until he died. The Qianlong emperor (r. 1736-1795) dared not to pollute his grandfather's former residence and converted it into rare books storage in order to show his reverence. In the ninth year of the Qianlong reign (1744) and the second year of the Jiaqing reign (1797), the rare books of the Song (960-1279), Liao (916-1125), Jin (1115-1234), Yuan (1271-1368) and Ming (1368-1644) dynasties were gathered into and preserved in the Hall. The plaque with the Qianlong emperor's inscription of "Tian Lu Lin Lang" (Beautiful Treasures of the Heaven) is hung on its wall.

The emperor's study in the Hall of Luminous Benevolence: storage of the Song (960-1279) and Yuan (1271-1368) books

The emperor's office and dining hall: the Hall of Expanding Virtue

The Hall of Expanding Virtue

The Ming and Qing emperors came to the Hall of Expanding Virtue very often. In the official Qing records, the Hall was known as the imperial office and dining room. On the New Year's Day, it was the very place for the Qing emperor to take dumplings. The more common activities carried out in the Hall, esp. in the Kangxi period (1662-1722), were academic discussions and lectures. When Emperor Tongzhi was young, the empress dowagers often came here to deal with state affairs. When Tongzhi reached school age, the Hall was converted into his study.

The symbol of peace between the Heaven and Earth: the Hall of Union and Peace

The Hall of Union and Peace

Located between the Palace of Heavenly Purity and the Palace of Earthly Tranquility, the Hall of Union and Peace implied that the union of the Heaven and the Earth would bring peace of *yang* and *yin* and expressed best wishes for the harmony of the emperor and the empress.

In the Hall, a plaque with the inscription of "Wu Wei" (Non Action) by Emperor Kangxi is hung above the throne. On the left is a water clock made in the Qianlong period (1736-1795); on the right is a chiming clock made by the Imperial Workshops in the Jiaqing period (1796-1820).

Water Clock in the Hall of Union and Peace

The Hall was the place for the empress to accept felicitations on festivals. In the Shunzhi period (1644-1661), an iron plate prohibiting the eunuchs from interfering in political affairs was set in the Hall in order to avoid the disadvantages of eunuch's seizing power in the former dynasty.

Twenty-Five Imperial Seals On both sides of the throne in the Hall of Union and Peace stand the 25 imperial seals symbolizing state power and selected in the 11th year of the Qianlong reign (1746). With different materials like gold, jade and sandalwood, the seals were meant for various purposes, such as issuing imperial edict, announcing the results of the Palace Examination, rewarding officials, etc.

Case storing one of the twenty-five imperial seals

The emperor's seal symbolizing imperial authority

The Palace of Earthly Tranquility with Manchu features

The Palace of Earthly Tranquility

The Palace of Earthly Tranquility was the residence of the Ming empress, who would live there from her wedding, if not deposed, until her death. After the Qing dominated the Central Plains, the Palace was re-structured according to the Manchu customs. The west part was used to offer sacrifices to the gods while the east part served as bridal chamber, where the imperial couple would stay for three days after wedding ceremony, in order to show the sublime position of the empress among imperial consorts.

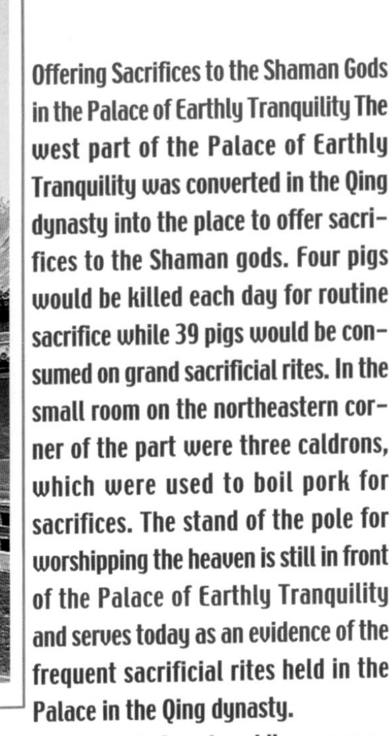

Offering Sacrifices to the Shaman Gods in the Palace of Earthly Tranquility The west part of the Palace of Earthly Tranquility was converted in the Qing dynasty into the place to offer sacrifices to the Shaman gods. Four pigs would be killed each day for routine sacrifice while 39 pigs would be consumed on grand sacrificial rites. In the small room on the northeastern corner of the part were three caldrons, which were used to boil pork for sacrifices. The stand of the pole for worshipping the heaven is still in front of the Palace of Earthly Tranquility and serves today as an evidence of the frequent sacrificial rites held in the Palace in the Qing dynasty.

Bridal Chamber of Imperial Couple Grand wedding ceremonies were held when the emperor married the empress. It was in the Palace of Earthly Tranquility that the Kangxi (r. 1662-1722), Tongzhi (r. 1862-1874) and Guangxu (r. 1875-1908) emperors drank the nuptial cups together with their empresses. The furnishings in the bridal chamber still retain the original style of the wedding of the Guangxu emperor. In the north of the chamber are two wood *kang* adorned with carved partitions, the west one was the dragon-and-phoenix bed of the new imperial couple since the Kangxi period. The bed is decorated with a curtain and a quilt with the design of dragons and phoenixes. On the upper panel of the bed

is hung the plaque with the inscription of "Ri Sheng Yue Geng" (Rising Sun and Waxing Moon) by Empress Dowager Cixi. When the empress entered the Palace, she would stride over a brazier, symbolizing "becoming more prosperous everyday". On the doorsill of the Palace was set a saddle and the empress would have the apple in her hand placed under the saddle, symbolizing "being peaceful all the time" as the combined pronunciation of apple and saddle is the same as the pronunciation of peace in Chinese.

The caldron for boiling meat and worshiping gods in the Palace of Earthly Tranquility

Splendid bridal chamber in the Palace of Earthly Tranquility

Schoolroom of the Qing Princes: the Upper Study

The Wings of the Palace of Heavenly Purity

The courtyard around the Palace of Heavenly Purity is the center of the Inner Court. In order to serve the emperor more timely and flexibly, the court set some service organs in the wings of the Palace. The east wing mainly serves the imperial life while the west wing acts as administrative offices.

The west wing shows an exhibition about the emperor's birthday celebrations today.

Upper Study

On the east of the Gate of Heavenly Purity was the Upper Study. After the Yongzheng emperor (r. 1723-1735) moved to the Hall of Mental Cultivation, he converted a room east to the Gate into the Upper

Reading notes of Yongyan (future Emperor Jiaqing) and his letter to his teacher

Study, so that he could examine the princes' study progress at any time. Those who were qualified to study there included his sons and grandsons as well as the male descendents of his close relatives. The teachers in this study could be divided into two categories: the Han Chinese teachers were called "mentors". As imperial scholars and prestigious ministers, they were entitled to sit in tall chairs in the study. The teachers who taught Manchu, Mongolian, riding and shooting were called "masters". Proficient in Manchu and good at riding and shooting, they were not allowed to sit before the imperial students. In addition, an important minister was appointed by the emperor as mentor general. He was above the mentors and responsible for the overall imperial education.

South Study

The South Study was the study of the Shunzhi and Kangxi emperors in their childhoods. At the age of 16, Emperor Kangxi subdued Aobai and took over the reins of government. After that, he selected erudite ministers from imperial scholars to work in the South Study, so that they could answer his questions at any time, thus starting the history of South Study as an organization in the Inner Court. Those who were selected into the Study were people with good character and fine scholarship and they became capable assistants of the emperor in dealing with specific matters. The imperial edicts were often drafted and the imperial calligraphic works rewarded to others were often written by them.

Duty room of imperial scholars: the South Study

It was in the South Study that Emperor Kangxi subdued the powerful minister Aobai, who was a valiant general of the early Qing dynasty. Before the Shunzhi emperor died, he named his third son eight-year-old Xuanye as his successor (i.e. the later Emperor Kangxi) and appointed Suoni, Sukesaha, Ebilong and Aobai as main ministers. Aobai seized the political power regardless of the young emperor and tried to get rid of his enemies. To slacken Aobai's vigilance, Kangxi played wrestling all day long with his young guards. One day, he asked Aobai to come to the Study alone and ordered his guards to subdue Aobai and send him to the Board of Punishments. At the same time, the Imperial Guards arrested Aobai's followers. After that, the Kangxi emperor took over the reins of the government.

Emperor Kangxi's inscription on a plaque, exhorting the eunuchs to serve the court diligently

The Room of Meticulous Working

In feudal China, the imperial servants were deprived of their reproductive ability and called eunuchs. Located in the west of the Gate of Heavenly Purity and east of the South Study, the Room of Meticulous Working was an organization in charge of eunuchs under the Imperial Household Department. A plaque with the inscription of "The Room of Meticulous Working" by Emperor Kangxi was hung in the Room.

In the Ming dynasty, eunuchs amounted to over 100,000 and

were notorious for interfering in state affairs. After the Qing dominated the Central Plains, the management of eunuchs was tightened and the amount of eunuchs was cut down to over 400 in the early Qing dynasty. In the 16th year of the Kangxi period (1677), the Room of Meticulous Working was set up to manage the 3,300 eunuchs in the imperial palace. The duties of the Room were miscellaneous, including controlling improper behaviors of the eunuchs, handling routine affairs, receiving and checking the revenue, dealing with the documents in the Imperial Household Department, examining the opening and closing of the gates and inspecting the safety of fire and candles, etc.

The vast difference of the numbers of eunuchs in the Ming and Qing dynasties is astonishing. According to relevant records, the Ming eunuchs amounted to over 100,000 while the number of eunuchs was over 400 in the early Qing. Even in the prime period of the Qianlong reign, there were 2,605 eunuchs in the Imperial Palace. But according to relevant regulations of the Qing dynasty, the number of eunuchs in the Imperial Palace should be 3,300.

The Place for Worshiping Confucius

Confucius was a famous philosopher in China. His philosophy known as Confucianism was held in great esteem by rulers of past dynasties. In a room at the southern end of the east wing of the Palace of Heavenly Purity was placed his memorial tablet with the inscription of "Yu Tian Di San" (Revered together with the Heaven and the Earth) by Emperor Qianlong, who came to

the Place to worship Confucius in the early morning of each New Year's Day. The Place was very near to the Upper Study. When a prince reached school age and came to the Study for the first time, he would burn incense sticks and worship Confucius in this Place.

Portrait of Confucius

Imperial Medicine Room

Located south to the Gate of Sun Essence, Imperial Medicine Room was mainly responsible for taking imperial doctors to see the patients in the Imperial Palace, having prescriptions made up and decocting medicinal herbs. The emperor managed the Medicine Room strictly. According to relevant regulations in the Yongzheng period (1723-1735), imperial medicine was very important and all the silver bottles and prescriptions should be marked clearly.

Under the Imperial Household

Shelves for storing medicines in Imperial Medicine Room

Pot for decocting medicine herbs in Imperial Medicine Room

Department, the Imperial Medicine Room should arrange imperial doctors to stay in the Imperial Palace at night, in order to meet the needs of the Inner Court at any time. Though the imperial doctors saw the imperial patients throughout the year, they were not allowed to disclose relevant information, because the physical conditions of the emperor had a great deal to do with the stability of the state.

There were over 400 precious medicines in the Imperial Medicine Room. Various pills, powders and ointments were made by imperial doctors and officials of the Imperial Medicine Room together, with one kept watch on another. The imperial medicines mainly came from the following channels: collected from provinces, purchased from markets in Beijing or presented by local officials as tributes.

Imperial Tea Room

Imperial Tea Room was a place to prepare tea, fruits and refreshments. The name of the Room was written by Emperor Kangxi (r. 1662-1722), inscribed on a plaque and hung in the Room. The water used to make tea was specially transported from the Hill of Jade Spring. The firewood for boiling the water amounted to 425 kilogram each day. The emperor was very particular about the quality of tea and water, esp. the water. Emperor Qianlong (r. 1736-1795) once sent people to use a specially made water measure to compare the springs all over China.

The Hall of Uprightness

The Hall of Uprightness is located in the center of the east wing of the Palace of Heavenly Purity. The name of the Hall means that the upright position of the emperor's crown would prevent temptation and help the emperor distinguish between right and wrong. That's why the Hall was used to store the emperor's crowns and hats.

The Place for Inner Report

The Place for Inner Report was the unit closest to the emperor and was the most important organization in the Inner Court. It is located south to the Gate of Moon Brilliance. Its major duties included proclaiming imperial edicts, leading the way for the ministers summoned by the emperor, dealing with various documents and serving the emperor at night. Due to their significant duties, the eunuchs in the Place tended to take bribes and bully people. In the Ming dynasty, head eunuchs like Wei Zhongxian and Wang An were so arrogant that they caused a lot of harms. The Qing took lessons from the Ming court and controlled the eunuchs strictly. That's why the disasters caused by the eunuchs never occurred in the Qing dynasty.

The cushion for officials of the Department of Military Affairs to kneel down and four treasures of the study (writing brush, ink stick, paper and ink stone) used by the emperor

The Hall of Diligence

The Hall of Diligence was the emperors' study and storage of their books, writings as well as painting and calligraphy collections, thus presenting a strong cultural atmosphere. But every autumn, the emperor would come here to go through a ritual that had nothing to do with cultural affairs, known as the "the ritual of crossing out", i.e. crossing out the names of those criminals who were guilty of the most heinous crimes and showed no sign of repentance with red writing brush and those criminals would be sent to the Board of Punishments for execution.

Antithetical couplet written by the Yongzheng emperor (r. 1723-1735)

Kangxi Dictionary

The Pavilion of Thousand Autumns

Imperial Garden

The Imperial Garden was known as the Garden behind the Palace and was changed to its current name in the Qing dynasty. It covers 12,000 square meters and accounts for 1.7% of the Forbidden City, in which there are four gardens, i.e. the Imperial Garden, the Garden of Benevolent Tranquility, the Garden of Creating Happiness and the Qianlong Garden. Among them, the Imperial Garden is the largest one.

The Imperial Garden was a place for the imperial family to take a rest and hold various activities to celebrate festivals.

The Imperial Garden was also a junction in the Inner Court: the Gate of Obedience and Chastity lies north to the big

The last empress Wanrong (middle) and imperial concubine Wenxiu (left) enjoying themselves in the Imperial Garden

The Hill of Accumulating Elegance

screen wall and south to the Square before the Gate of Spiritual Valor. The Garden's south gate, the Gate of Earthly Tranquility, is the entrance of the Three Rear Palaces. The West Gate of Jeweled Garden in the southwest is the portal to the Six Western Palaces while the East Gate of Jeweled Garden in the southeast is the portal to the Six Eastern Palaces.

@ Links

Three Grotesque Rocks in the Imperial Garden

There are 45 miniature rocks in the Imperial Garden, and most of them are made of taihu rocks. Among them, the strangest ones are known as "Three Grotesque Rocks", i.e. sea cucumber rock, the rock with the natural pattern of worshipping the Big Dipper and fossil wood. The former two rocks lie on both sides of the Gate of Water while the latter one is placed before the Lodge of Crimson Snow.

The sea cucumber rock is 78 cm long, 66 cm wide and 14 cm thick. It consists of numerous sea-cucumber-shaped small rocks and forms a natural table screen. Though they are not fossils, the crisscross sea cucumbers look so vivid that they seem smooth and soft. However, their quality is pretty hard.

The rock with the pattern of worshipping the

Fossil wood

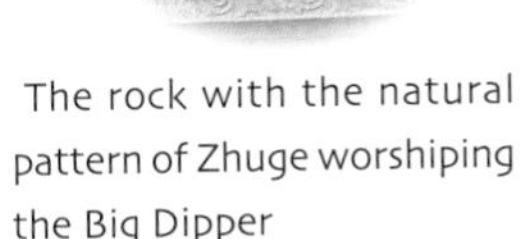

The rock with the natural pattern of Zhuge worshiping the Big Dipper

Sea cucumber rock

Big Dipper is 50 cm long, 42 cm wide and 29 cm thick. It is marked with the naturally formed pattern of a Daoist with long robe and wide sleeves worshipping the Big Dipper.
The fossil looks like a wood with clear veins. It is 130 cm long, 27 cm wide and 10 cm thick, and stands on a lotus-shaped marble stand. It was presented by Heilongjiang General Fuseng'e in the Qianlong period (1736-1795). Emperor Qianlong liked it so much that he wrote an ode and had the ode inscribed on it.

The Lodge of Crimson Snow

The Lodge of Crimson Snow was a favorite study of Emperor Qianlong. Its name came from the five crabapple trees grown in front of the Lodge. Unfortunately, they were substituted in the late Qing dynasty by mock oranges, which, together with peonies, symbolize peace and prosperity and create the auspicious atmosphere peculiar to imperial garden.

Picture of the last emperor Puyi, his brother Pujie, his brother-in-law Runqi and his tutor Reginald Fleming Johnston

Cypresses with Entwined Branches

Most cypresses in the Imperial Garden were grown in the Ming dynasty. They, as evergreens, are indispensable in decorating gardens. Their branches have the same pronunciation as "hundred sons". Cypresses were planted extensively in the Garden so as to bless the imperial family with flourishing posterity. There are many trees with entwined branches in the Imperial Garden. The cypresses with entwined branches before the Hall of Imperial Peace are the most spectacular. The two cypresses have different roots but share the same crown. The entwined branches symbolize the everlasting love of a couple. They have a history of three or four hundred years.

Picture of the last emperor Puyi (middle) and his brother Pujie in front of the cypresses with branches entwined together

Picture of the last emperor Puyi taken after being restored to power in 1917 (the restoration lasted only 12 days) in front of the cypresses with branches entwined together

The Hall of Imperial Peace: the place to worship Daoism in the Imperial Palace

The Hall of Imperial Peace

The Hall of Imperial Peace enshrined the God of Murky Warrior in Daoism, i.e. the Water God and Guardian Spirit of the North. As the architecture in the Forbidden City is mainly made of wood, the Water God was devoutly worshiped in order to prevent fires. Especially as great fires often broke out in the Imperial Palace in the Jiajing period (1522-1566), the Jiajing emperor believed in Daoism piously and worshiped the God of Murky Warrior as fire suppressor. He also had "Tian Yi Zhi Men" inscribed on the front gate of the Hall's enclosed walls. The words were excerpted from *The Book of Changes*, blessing the Forbidden City to be free from fire.

The gilded *kylin* symbolizing majesty of Daoism placed before the Gate of Water

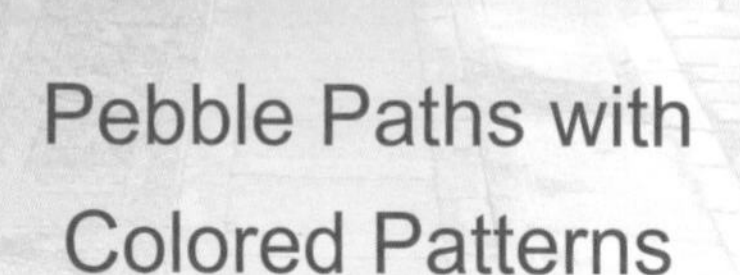

Pebble Paths with Colored Patterns

The paths in the Imperial Garden are paved with pebbles with various colors and consist of over 900 patterns, telling traditional stories popular in China. They are noted for exquisite craftsmanship and vivid designs.

Guan and Huang fighting with swords: a pattern on the pebble path in the Imperial Garden

The West Route

The Map of the West Route

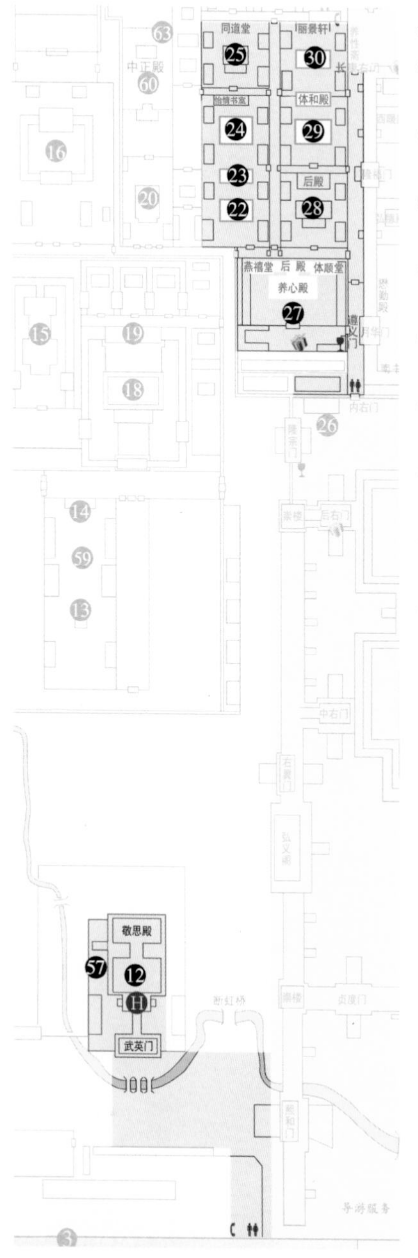

- 12 The Hall of Military Glory
- 22 The Hall of Ultimate Supremacy
- 23 The Hall of All-Encompassing Universe
- 24 The Palace of Everlasting Spring
- 25 The Palace of Universal Happiness
- 27 The Hall of Mental Cultivation
- 28 The Palace of Eternal Longevity
- 29 The Palace of Assisting the Earth
- 30 The Palace of Concentrated Beauty
- 57 The Chamber of Immersing in Virtue

The West Route mainly covers the Six Western Palaces and the Hall of Mental Cultivation. The Six Western Palaces include the Pălace of Eternal Longevity, the Hall of Ultimate Supremacy, the Palace of Everlasting Spring, the Palace of Assisting the Earth, the Palace of Concentrated Beauty and the Palace of Universal Happiness. They were residences of imperial consorts. The Hall of Mental Cultivation had been the political center of the Qing dynasty since the Yongzheng period. Eight Qing emperors lived and worked there and many historic events also took place there, e.g. holding court behind a curtain and abdication of the last emperor.

The imperial consorts of the Ming and Qing lived in the Six Eastern Palaces and Six Western Palaces. While the former remain the original style of the Yongle period, the latter were rebuilt in a large scale in the Qing dynasty. The united and symmetrical structure was changed greatly. For example, the Gate of Concentrated Beauty was dismantled to build a five-bay hall with corridors, the Hall of Manifesting Harmony. The Gate of Everlasting Spring was dismantled to build a five-bay hall with a stage, the Hall of All-Encompassing Universe.

The Hall of Mental Cultivation is located south to the Six Western Palaces. One would come to the Square before the Gate of Heavenly Purity after crossing the Right Gate of the Inner Court in the south, would come to the Imperial Garden after crossing the West Gate of Jeweled Garden in the north and would come to the Palace of Heavenly Purity after crossing the Gate of Moon Brilliance in the east.

The Palace of Concentrated Beauty was Cixi's residence when she first entered the Imperial Palace. The current exhibits on display reflect the original state when Cixi celebrated her 50th birthday.

The Palace of Concentrated Beauty

In the Ming dynasty, the Palace of Concentrated Beauty was an ordinary palace. It became very famous in the late Qing dynasty as the place of origin of Empress Dowager Cixi.

Cixi, néeYehenala and pet named Lan'er (Orchid), was a concubine of Emperor Xianfeng (r. 1851-1861). She came from the Bordered Blue Banner (a political and military organization of Manchu) and was raised to Bordered Yellow Banner after becoming Empress Dowager. In February 1852, 18-year-old Lan'er entered the Palace and was conferred with the title of "Honorable Person Orchid". Her first residence in the Imperial Palace was the Palace of Concentrated Beauty, and it was in this Palace that she gave birth to her son and the only son of Emperor Xianfeng, Zaichun. After Emperor Xianfeng died, her six-year-old son became Emperor Tongzheng (r. 1862-1874) and she became Empress Dowager Cixi. She began holding court behind a curtain together with Emperor Xianfeng's empress, Empress Dowager Ci'an and ruled over China for 48 years.

In the tenth year of the Guangxu reign (1884), the Qing court spent 630,000 taels of silver to renovate the Palace of Concentrated Beauty, in order to celebrate the 50th birthday of Empress Dowager Cixi. The Palace became the most luxurious palace in the Inner Court, the walls of whose corridors are inlaid with blue glass swastikas and inscribed with *Odes to Longevity* presented by officials.

Empress Dowager Cixi

The Lodge of Beautiful Landscape behind the Palace is now the exhibition gallery showing the life of Puyi.

The Hall of Manifesting Harmony

On each side of the front steps before the Hall of Manifesting Harmony stands a bronze phoenix. The inscription on the plaque of the Hall "Xiang Feng Wei Lin" means that the owner of the Hall lives together with phoenixes. It was in this Hall that Emperor Guangxu selected his empress and imperial concubines. The plaque with the inscription of "Ti Yi Bao Yuan" written by Empress Dowager Cixi is hung in the Hall. When Empress Dowager Cixi lived in the Palace of Concentrated Beauty, the Hall was used as her dining hall.

Bronze phoenix and crane before the Hall of Assisting the Earth, symbolizing the virtue of and best wishes for imperial consort

The Palace of Assisting the Earth

In this Palace built in the Ming dynasty, Emperor Wanli (r. 1573-1620) and his favorite concubine Zheng were in deep love with each other for over 40 years.

Zheng was an ordinary imperial maid. Emperor Wanli fell in love with her as soon as he saw her and conferred the title of "honorable concubine" upon her. In order to designate Zheng's son as crown prince, Wanli ignored the existence of his eldest son and argued with his ministers for several decades. Due to the strong resistance of the ministers, the emperor only conferred the title of Prince Happiness upon his beloved son, who died tragically: when the Ming fell down, he was captured and eaten by peasant insurgents.

The imperial concubine of the last emperor Wenxiu also lived in this Palace. In 1931, this self-respected concubine strived for her rights of equality and freedom by divorcing Puyi and earned her own living via teaching.

The Palace of Everlasting Spring

The Palace of Everlasting Spring was the residence of Emperor Qianlong's beloved wife Empress Xiaoxian, who died when she was only 37 years old. The Emperor was so sad that he ordered not to change the original state of her residence. Just before he died, he allowed imperial consorts of later generations to live in it.

Last emperor's concubine Wenxiu (right) and her open-minded sister

Exquisite furnishings in the Palace of Everlasting Spring

The walls of its corridors are decorated with over ten paintings with the themes selected from *The Dream of Red Mansions*, an important novel in Chinese literary history. These paintings were proposed by Concubine Zhen of Emperor Guangxu and created with western perspective principle and Chinese painting techniques. Characterized by well-knit composition and elegant style, the paintings display superb craftsmanship and look very spectacular.

The painting of *The Dream of Red Mansions* on the walls of the corridors before the Palace of Everlasting Spring

Interior of the Hall of Ultimate Supremacy

The Hall of Ultimate Supremacy

The Hall of Ultimate Supremacy was a quiet and elegant palace. The father of Emperor Jiajing was born here. After Jiajing (r. 1522-1566) became emperor, he insisted upon admitting his father posthumously as Emperor Xingxian and changed the name of his father's birthplace to the Palace of Originating Auspiciousness. The Wanli emperor (r. 1573-1620) moved to the Hall after the Palace of Heavenly Purity was burned down and once summoned ministers here for consultation.

Plaque of the Palace of Eternal Longevity

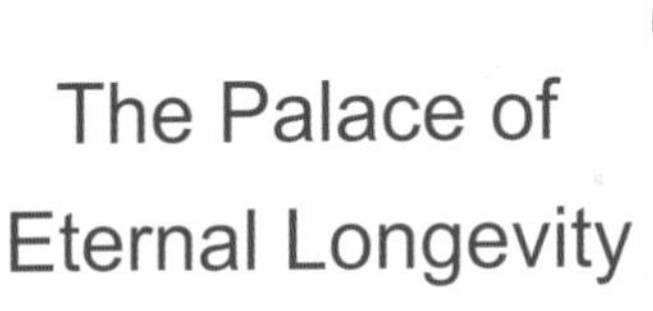

The Palace of Eternal Longevity

The Palace of Eternal Longevity was the very place where the mother of Emperor Hongzhi died suddenly and mysteriously. In the Qing dynasty, due to the Palace's close distance to the Palace of Benevolent Tranquility and the Hall of Mental Cultivation, the Palace was often used to give banquets. For example, when Emperor Qianlong's favorite daughter Princess Hexiao got married, imperial banquet was given and court music was played there.

The emperors in ancient China had numerous consorts, and there was a saying of "three palaces, six courtyards and 72 concubines". However, the number of Ming and Qing concubines did not reach this amount, e.g. Emperor Kangxi (r. 1662-1722) had 55 concubines. By the time of the Guangxu period (1875-1908), the Emperor had only one empress and two concubines.

As the Inner Court was the residence of imperial consorts and the place to give birth to princes and princesses, the plaques of palaces and gates in it have something to do with how to be a dutiful wife and good mother. The examples are the Palace of Obeying the Heaven, the Palace of Assisting the Earth, the Gate of Thousand Babies, the Gate of Hundred Sons, etc.

The Palace of Universal Happiness

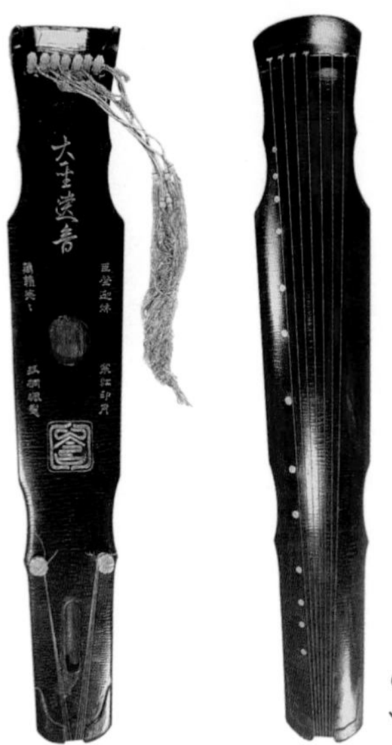

Qin with the inscription of "Da Sheng Yi Yin" (Music Left Behind by the Saint)

The Palace of Universal Happiness is located in the northwest of the Six Western Palaces. It was the very place where Emperor Qianlong (1736-1795) burned incense and played the *qin*. In the east wing of the Palace, the Emperor preserved several precious *qin*, among which the most famous ones are "Singing of Phoenix" of the Song (960-1279) and "Immortal Music" of the Ming (1368-1644). The Emperor loved the *qin* so much that he wrote the plaque

"The Lodge of the *Qin* Virtue" himself. In the Jiaqing (1796-1820) and Daoguang (1821-1850) periods, the emperors lived in the Palace for certain days after their fathers died.
Now the Palace is used to display an exhibition on the coup d'état of Xinyou.

The Hall of Mental Cultivation

The Hall of Mental Cultivation occupied a very important position in the Qing history. It was the very place that Shunzhi (r. 1644-1661), Qianlong (r. 1736-1795) and Tongzhi (r. 1862-1874) emperors died. After Emperor Yongzheng (r. 1723-1735) moved here, the Hall of Mental Cultivation became imperial office and residence, i.e. the political, military and cultural center of the Qing dynasty.

The Hall of Mental Cultivation was the political center of the Qing dynasty.

The emperor's dragon bed

The Hall of Mental Cultivation is shaped like "工" and consists of two parts. The front part was the emperor's office. The plaque "Zhongzheng Renhe" (Just and Benevolent) written by Emperor Yongzheng (r. 1723-1735) is hung in the Hall. On the New Year's Day every year, the emperor would hold a ritual before the southern window of the east part of the Hall called "start writing before bright window" by writing down some auspicious words. After Emperor Xianfeng (1851-1861) died, the east part of the Hall was converted into the place for holding court behind the curtain. On 12 February 1912, the last Qing empress dowager Longyu signed the last imperial edict of the Great Qing on behalf of the six-year-old Emperor Xuantong, announcing his abdication.

The west part of the Hall was used by the emperor to summon his ministers for consulting key political and military affairs and dealing with routine matters. In order to guarantee secrecy, the terrace before this part of the Hall is enclosed with thick red panels. In the late Qing dynasty, it was in this part of the Hall that Empress Dowagers Cixi and Ci'an decided that the son of

Prince Chun Zaitian would be the future emperor. Prince Chun cried on the spot and then lost his consciousness.

The back part of the Hall was the emperor's residence and consists of five rooms separated with finely carved phoebe *nanmu* partitions and decorated with luxurious furnishings. The emperor had two beds: the eastern one is inlaid with glass mirrors and adorned with exquisite sachets; the western one is covered with red felt and yellow blanket and was usually the very bed where the emperor spent the night with one of his consorts, who would be chosen by the emperor at dinnertime by turning over the tablet with her name. The eunuch in charge would inform her to come to the Hall to serve the emperor at night.

The last emperor Puyi in the Hall of Mental Cultivation

The emperor's living room in the Back Hall of Mental Cultivation

Furnishings in the Back Hall of Mental Cultivation

To Boyuan was the only authentic calligraphic masterpiece left behind by the Jin literati among the three rare treasures.

The Room of Three Rare Treasures in the Hall of Mental Cultivation, the very place for Emperor Qianlong to admire antiquities

Links

The Room of Three Rare Treasures The westernmost room of the Hall of Mental Cultivation is the Room of Three Rare Treasures. The no more than four-square-meter room was used by the Qianlong emperor to store his favorite calligraphic masterpieces, i.e., *Clear Up after Snow* by Wang Xizhi, *Mid Autumn* by Wang Xianzhi and *To Boyuan* by Wang Xun. The name of the room was written by Qianlong and hung as a plaque on the east wall of the Room.

The three rare treasures are now preserved in the Palace Museums in Beijing and Taipei.

Holding Court behind a Curtain The east part of the Hall of Mental Cultivation is noted for "holding court behind a curtain". After Emperor Xianfeng (1851-1861) died in the Summer Mountain Retreat in 1861, his two consorts Cixi and Ci'an united his brother Prince Gong to stage a coup d'état and beat their political enemies. On 1 November, Cixi began holding court behind a curtain and started her 48-year rule of China.

East Part of the Hall of Mental Cultivation, the very place where Cixi held the court behind a curtain

The Hall of Military Glory

The Hall of Military Glory is situated on the west of the Hall of Supreme Harmony. In the Ming Dynasty, the emperor stayed here for fast and often visited this informal hall; the empress also accepted the felicitations from titled ladies here on her birthday. In the Kangxi period (1662-1722), a publishing house was set up here. In the Qianlong period (1736-1795), it was used for carving and printing "Palace Books", the most precious official books.

In September 2005, it became a painting gallery and exhibition place showing the Palace Books.

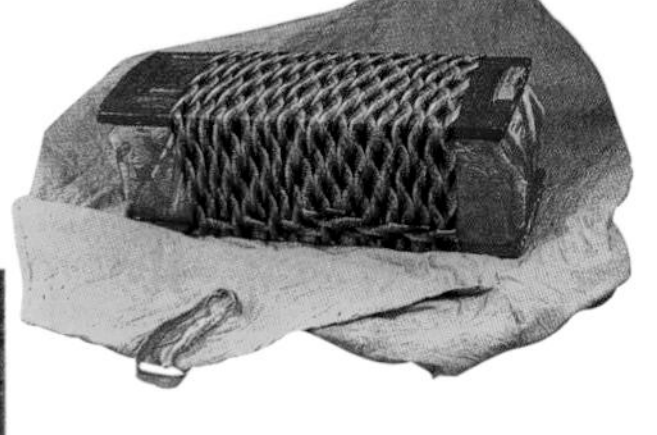

The *Manchu Kangyur*

The original printing blocks of the *Manchu Kangyur*

The Hall of Military Glory was the imperial press. The Palace Books printed there are very precious.

The Chamber of Immersing in Virtue

Located behind the Hall of Military Glory, the Chamber of Immersing in Virtue is marked with Turkish style. Under a towering dome, its interior walls are covered with white glazed tiles. It is said that Concubine Fragrance, the Uigur concubine of Emperor Qianlong, once lived here. According to textual research, it was originally a bathroom in the Construction Department outside the Gate of Worshipping the Heaven, the front gate of the Yuan imperial palace. This building with Turkish style was kept when the Forbidden City was built in the Yongle period of the Ming dynasty.

The interior of the Chamber of Immersing in Virtue

The East Route

The Map of the East Route

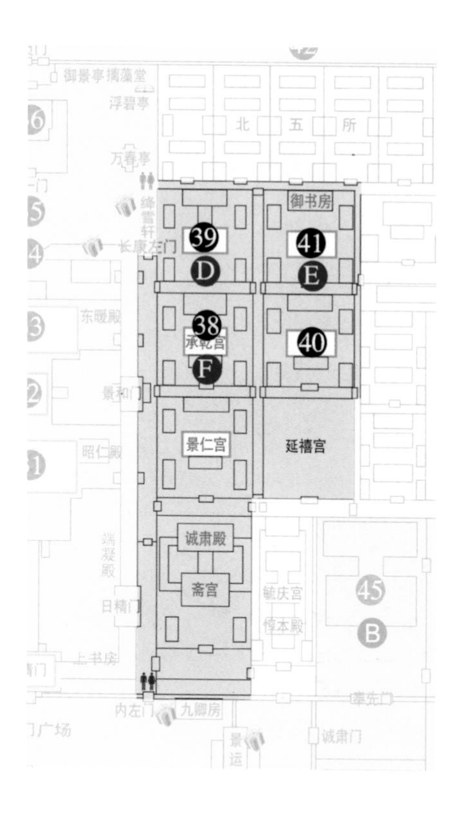

38 The Palace of Obeying the Heaven

39 The Palace of Cherishing Essence

40 The Palace of Eternal Harmony

41 The Palace of Revering Yang

The major tourist attractions in the East Route are the Six Eastern Palaces and the Palace of Abstinence. The Six Eastern Palaces include the Palace of Cherishing Essence, the Palace of Obeying the Heaven, the Palace of Revering Benevolence, the Palace of Revering *Yang*, the Palace of Eternal Harmony and the Palace of Extending Happiness. In general, these Palaces remain the original Ming style and are separate courtyards. Every courtyard is square, covering an area of 2,500 square meters. They are now exhibition galleries of the Palace Museum.

In the Ming dynasty, the empress lived in the Palace of Earthly Tranquility, which was known as the Main Palace or Central Palace. The other imperial consorts lived in the Six Eastern Palaces and Six Western Palaces. In the Qing dynasty, after the wedding nights with the emperor in the Palace of Earthly Tranquility, the empress could choose any one among the Six Eastern Palaces and Six Western Palaces as her daily residence. The high-ranking imperial consorts like the empress and imperial honorable concubine were entitled to have their own palaces while the consorts at lower levels had to share a palace with others.

Out of the Left Gate of the Inner Court, the Square before the Gate of Heavenly Purity is to the south of the Six Eastern Palaces. Out of the East Gate of Jeweled Garden, the Imperial Garden is to the north of the Six Eastern Palaces. You can also reach the Palace of Heavenly Purity through the Gate of Sun Essence.

Tranquil courtyard in the Palace of Cherishing Essence

The Palace of Cherishing Essence

The Palace of Cherishing Essence was the residence for the crown prince in the Ming dynasty. Emperors Xianfeng and Tongzhi of the Qing dynasty also lived here when they were princes.

The Palace of Cherishing Essence became an important residence for empresses and concubines in the late Qing dynasty. It was the Main Palace of Empress Xiaozhenxian, wife of Emperor Xianfeng, the future Empress Dowager Ci'an and also the Main Palace of Empress Longyu, wife of Emperor Guangxu. Both empresses led sad lives. They became

Portrait of Empress Dowager Ci'an in casual dress

widows in their twenties and thirties and suffered deaths in their forties.

The Ming buildings are not commonly seen now in the Palace Museum. But the Palace of Cherishing Essence will remind you of the old days. The main wooden structure of the Palace beams was built in the early Ming dynasty. Some colored paintings of the Ming dynasty still survive today after changes of dynasties and many restorations.

The Jade Gallery of the Palace Museum is now in the Palace of Cherishing Essence.

The Palace of Revering *Yang*

The Palace of Revering *Yang* was once the Concubine Prison in the Ming dynasty. A poor woman abandoned by Emperor Wanli gave birth here to Zhu Changluo, the future Emperor Guangzong. She cried to blindness and left the world before the enthronement of her beloved son.

In the Qing dynasty, the Palace of Revering *Yang* became a library of precious books, where emperors often dropped by to read at their leisure. It is now the Gallery of Enamel and Cloisonné. The remains of the old imperial library can still be detected here in the Palace.

The serene Palace of Revering *Yang* is telling the past glory and sadness.

The front hall of the Palace of Obeying the Heaven, where Concubine Dong' e, the beloved woman of Emperor Shunzhi lived.

The Palace of Obeying the Heaven

In the early Qing dynasty, the first hostess of the Palace of Obeying the Heaven was Dong'e, beloved concubine of Emperor Shunzhi. She was daughter of Eshuo, the Deputy Head of Imperial Troops and was of Plain White Banner, Manchu origin. Dong'e originally was wife of Prince Bomuboguo'er, younger brother of Emperor Shunzhi. The Emperor's extraordinary love for his sister-in-law led to the suicide of Prince Bomuboguo'er. Emperor Shunzhi then married his sister-in-law and entitled her as Imperial Honorable Concubine. The couple was very much in love. However, the young death of their child broke the heart of Dong'e. She passed away out of sadness. The emperor was so grieved that he wanted to become a monk after her death. He issued an imperial edict to declare her

Portrait of Emperor Shunzhi in ceremonial robe

posthumously as the Empress Xiaoxianduanjing and a grand ceremony was held for this special occasion. The emperor lost all his interest in the world ever since and died soon after the death of his beloved.

The Palace of Obeying Heaven is now the Gallery of Bronzes.

The Palace of Eternal Harmony

Emperor Yongzheng, a reforming statesman in the Qing dynasty

Among all the consorts who lived in the Palace of Eternal Harmony, the Honorable Concubine De of Emperor Kangxi had most extraordinary experience. She had been living in the Palace of Eternal Harmony since the very moment she entered the Forbidden City. She gave birth here to the fourth prince Yinzhen (future Emperor Yongzheng) and the fourteenth prince Yinti. After her eldest son became emperor, she refused to move to the Palace of Benevolent Tranquility to enjoy the dignity an empress dowager should have enjoyed and died suddenly in the Palace of Eternal Harmony. The sudden death was left behind as a mysterious case in the history of the Qing Inner Court.

The Palace of Revering Benevolence

The Palace of Revering Benevolence was rebuilt during the reign of Emperor Shunzhi in the Qing dynasty. There is a white marble screen right behind the gate, which was said to be relics of the Yuan dynasty. The surface of the screen is covered with misty patterns of clouds and mountains, just like a witness to the history of the Palace. Emperor Kangxi was born and lived his unhappy childhood here. Concubine Zhen of Emperor Guangxu in the late Qing dynasty also lived here. Her life ended in tragedy. The Palace of Revering Benevolence now becomes a Memorial Hall for the Donators to show to the public the great contributions those people made to the Palace Museum and to display the valuable works of art they donated.

The Palace of Revering Benevolence collects all happy and sad stories.

The Palace of Extending Happiness

In the early years of Daoguang reign, several insignificant consorts of the Emperor lived here. One of them was Changzai (the seventh imperial consort entitled Being There All the Time) Lin.

Though her position was very low, she gave birth to Yi Xuan, the seventh prince, who was the father of Emperor Guangxu and grandfather of Emperor Xuantong.

It was said that this Palace was with no blessings and often caught fire without reasons. In 1845, the 25th year of the Daoguang reign, one big fire burned it down to dust. *Fengshui* practitioners were invited to the Palace and concluded that the bad location of the Palace caused the endless lightening strikes. They suggested not rebuilding the Palace in the same location. Therefore, there was no construction on this site any more during the reigns of Emperor Daoguang and Emperor Xianfeng.

This Palace has become the research centers of ceramics, paintings and calligraphy.

The Concubine Dowager Duankang (Concubine Jin, in the middle) watching fish in the Palace of Extending Happiness

The Palace of Abstinence

The Palace of Abstinence

The Palace of Abstinence was built in 1731, the 9th year of the Yongzheng reign. It was a ritual for the emperor to fast 3 days in the Palace of Abstinence before he offered sacrifice to the Heaven and Earth. The offer of sacrifice to the Heaven and Earth was a very important ritual in ancient Chinese sacrificial system and was listed as a grand state ceremony. Sometimes, the emperor would walk to the Temple of Heaven to pay his respects. Before the Sacrifice Ceremony, the emperor should hold the special "Abstinence Ceremony": There was another abstinence plate standing on the terrace before the Palace of Abstinence with a small bronze figure standing beside it holding an abstinence plate in his hands. The emperor should also carry a jade abstinence plate with him. The courtiers who joined the emperor in the ceremony all carried with them the abstinence plates made of different materials.

It is now a temporary exhibition gallery of the Palace Museum.

The Outer East Route

The Map of The Outer East Route

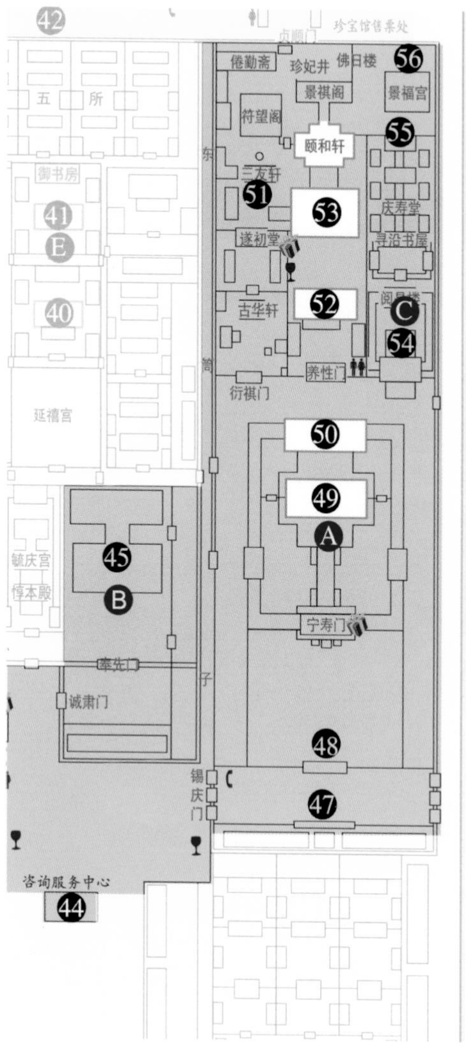

44 Arrow Pavilion

45 The Hall of Ancestral Worship

47 Nine Dragon Screen

48 The Gate of Imperial Supremacy

49 The Hall of Imperial Supremacy

50 The Palace of Tranquil Longevity

51 The Qianlong Garden

52 The Hall of Character Cultivation

53 The Chamber of Joyful Longevity

54 The Tower of Pleasant Sounds

55 The Courtyard for Celebrating Longevity

56 The Building of Buddhist Brilliance

The main spectacles in the Outer East Route are the Hall of Ancestral Worship outside the Gate of Prospering Fortune and the Complex of Tranquil Longevity (the Gallery of Treasures). They were the Hall of Benevolent Longevity and the Palace of Singing Phoenix, the residences for Grand Empress Dowagers, Empress Dowagers and Concubine Dowagers in the Ming dynasty. In 1689, Emperor Kangxi built the Palace of Tranquil Longevity on the site for Empress Dowager Xiaohuizhang, the empress of Shunzhi. In 1772, Emperor Qianlong decided to make this area his residence after retirement (as Super-Sovereign) and rebuilt it in accordance with the traditional layout of "court in the front and residence behind". Therefore, the architectural class of this palace was greatly raised. It became a city within the Forbidden City.

The Hall of Ancestral Worship, which is the family temple where the Qing emperors paid homage to their ancestors, is outside the Gate of Prospering Fortune if you start from the Square before the Gate of Heavenly Purity. The Complex of Tranquil Longevity is on the east of the Hall of Ancestral Worship. This Palace Complex is well organized, precisely composed and elegantly arranged. The Hall of Imperial Supremacy is an equivalent of the Palace of Heavenly Purity, residence of the Emperor but it copied the Hall of Supreme Harmony in the architectural form. Behind it is the Palace of Tranquil Longevity, a special place for sacrifice and a copy of the Palace of Earthy Tranquility in the architectural form. The well-known "Screen Wall of Nine Dragons" is facing the Gate of Imperial Supremacy.

The latter part of the Complex of Tranquil Longevity was designed for the leisure of the Super-Sovereign. There are the Garden of Tranquil Longevity (the Qianlong Garden), the Tower of Pleasant Sounds and the Building of Buddhist Brilliance.

The Hall of Character Cultivation in the middle route of the

Complex was a copy of the Hall of Mental Cultivation as the office of the Super-Sovereign. The following Chamber of Joyful Longevity, the Lodge for Cultivating Harmony and the Pavilion of Revering Goodness were intended as residences for him. However, in reality, he never lived here, but Empress Dowager Cixi in the late Qing dynasty often used the area as a temporary residence. The Complex of Tranquil Longevity still keeps its original look in the Qianlong period (1736-1795) and is now the Gallery of Treasures and Gallery of Stone Drums.

The splendid Screen Wall of Nine Dragons

The Screen Wall of Nine Dragons

There are three large Screen Walls of Nine Dragons in China. The earliest one was built in the Ming dynasty in Datong, Shangxi province. The other two are in Beijing: One is in Beihai Park (the Park of North Lake) with carvings on both sides; another one is in the Palace Museum. Covered with 270 glazed tiles, it is 71.6 meters long, 2.94 meters wide and 3.5 meters high. On the surface of the wall, nine vivid dragons are flying over seas and cliffs in different forms. The yellow dragon in the middle is directly facing the Gate of Imperial Supremacy and gazing at the Hall of Imperial Supremacy along the imperial route, thus increasing the majestic atmosphere.

The Hall of Ancestral Worship

The Hall of Ancestral Worship was built in the early Ming and rebuilt in 1656, the 13th year of the Shunzhi reign. It was the family temple where emperors could offer sacrifice to their

The Hall of Ancestral Worship

ancestors. The Emperor and Empress would come and pay homage here in every important festival. The Emperor also came here on the anniversaries of the deaths of his father and mother to show his sadness and memory. In addition, before the wedding ceremony, the Emperor would report here to his ancestors the background and character of the new empress and would take her to pay homage here to the ancestors after the Wedding Ceremony.

It is now the Gallery of Clocks and Watches.

Arrow Pavilion

Arrow Pavilion

Manchu started their rule of China with equitation and archery. Though living in the Forbidden City, the Qing Emperor ordered not to forget the old traditions. The Arrow Pavilion was built outside the Gate of Prospering Fortune to remind the descendents not to forget that their ancestors won the Country on horseback and to keep field practice. It is here that emperors reviewed the Imperial Martial Arts Examination.

The Arrow Pavilion is now the Visitor Center of the Palace Museum.

The Hall of Imperial Supremacy and The Palace of Tranquil Longevity

The Hall of Imperial Supremacy and the Palace of Tranquil Longevity are the largest buildings in this area with splendid and fresh-looking interior decoration. It was here that Emperor Kangxi (r. 1662-1722) served Empress Dowager Xiaohuizhang till her death, who was not his own mother and just 13 years older than him. In the Qianlong period (1736-1795), the Palace of Tranquil Longevity was renamed as the Hall of Imperial Supremacy and its back hall became the Palace of Tranquil Longevity. On 4 January of the first year of the Jiaqing reign (1796), Qianlong at the year of 85 held a grand banquet for thousands of old men in the Hall of Imperial Supremacy.

The Palace of Tranquil Longevity

The Hall of Character Cultivation was used as the place for receiving foreign envoys in the late Qing dynasty.

The Hall of Character Cultivation

The Hall of Character Cultivation was intended as the office of the Super-Sovereign, a copy of the Hall of Mental Cultivation in the architectural form. Before the 60th year of Qianlong reign (1795), he often gave internal banquets here to share happiness with important courtiers. In the late Qing dynasty, Empress Dowager Cixi used to dine here and received many foreign envoys and their wives in the Hall.

It is now the exhibition gallery of Golden Bells and Jade Chime.

Interior view of the top floor in the Tower of Pleasant Sounds

Interior view of the middle floor in the Tower of Pleasant Sounds

The Tower of Pleasant Sounds

Built in 1776, the 41st year of Qianlong's reign, the Tower of Pleasant Sounds has a history of more than 200 years. As the largest theater in the Imperial Palace, it is 21 meters high, covering an area of 690 square meters with 3 floors. The top floor was named "the floor of happiness", the one in the middle was called "the floor of prosperity" and the ground floor was "the floor of longevity", indicating the auspicious wishes of "happiness, prosperity and longevity." The emperor would sit in the center of the Building of Watching Operas, which is facing the Tower of Pleasant Sound from 10 meters away. The Building of Watching Operas was flanked by corridors connecting the Tower of Pleasant Sounds, where seated the courtiers and royal family.

The Building is now the gallery for the permanent exhibition of Qing Court Operas.

The Tower of Pleasant Sounds: the largest opera theater in the Forbidden City

The Chamber of Joyful Longevity

The Chamber of Joyful Longevity was planned to be the bedchamber for the Super-Sovereign. However, he never lived here. Empress Dowager Cixi used the west part of the Chamber as her bedroom and it was from here that she walked through to the back yard and ordered eunuchs to push and drown Concubine Zhen in the well. There is a throne in the center of the Chamber of Joyful Longevity for accepting felicitations. In the Chamber, there are jade boulders named "Mountain of Longevity" and "Sea of Happiness". Each weighs thousands of *jin* and was made out of the precious jade found in Hetian, Xinjiang in 1780, the 45th year of the Qianlong reign.

The Chamber of Joyful Longevity

The Well of Concubine Zhen

The Well of Concubine Zhen

A small house north to the Pavilion of Revering Goodness is where Concubine Zhen was confined by Empress Dowager Cixi. If you go through a small door, you will see the Well of Concubine Zhen where she was drowned to death.

Concubine Zhen was the beloved concubine of Emperor Guangxu. Because of supporting the Reform of Guangxu, she was in serious conflict with Cixi and was put into confinement and not allowed to meet the Emperor. When the Allied Forces of Eight Powers stormed into Beijing, Empress Dowager Cixi ordered eunuchs to push Concubine Zhen into this well and drown her before leaving Beijing. This Well was then named the Well of Concubine Zhen as a memorial.

The portrait of Concubine Zhen

The Qianlong Garden

Going through the Gate of Inheriting Goodness, there is an artificial rockery in front blocking the view. If you walk forward along the meandering pebble path, you will probably feel like heading for quiet seclusion. There is a square pavilion surrounded by trees behind the artificial rockery. It is named the Lodge of Ancient Tree. To the west, there is the elegant Pavilion of Ceremonial Purification. On the stone stele inside the Pavilion, there is the inscription of *Records of the Gathering at Orchid Pavilion* after Dong Qichang by Emperor Qianlong. On the floor, there is a meandering water channel. In ancient China, people believed that all the disasters and bad luck in the past year could go away if you take a bath in the river in the third day of the third month of Chinese lunar calendar. Wang Xizhi, a great calligrapher in the Easten Jin dynasty (317-420) wrote the famous *Prologue for the Gathering at Orchid Pavilion* when he was drinking with friends in the river while taking bath. From then on, ceremonial purification became a fashion in the circle of literati.

The water channel for floating cup in the
Pavilion of Ceremonial Purification

Exhibition Galleries

The collections in the Palace Museum can be regarded as a treasury of oriental civilization and a historical witness to the development of human civilization. It inherits the rich cultural heritages of ancient China and embodies the development of 5, 000 years of Chinese civilization. Among more than 1 million precious objects in the Palace Museum, there are bronze, ceramics, jade, paintings, calligraphy, enamel and cloisonné, lacquer, embroidery, gold and silver, sculpture, jewelry, bamboo and ivory carvings and furniture. Their value as antiques and historical witnesses could not be simply judged by valuation. A very small yet representative part of the collections is selected to display in different exhibition galleries.

The Gallery of Treasures

The Gallery of Treasures is located in the Complex of Tranquil Longevity in the Outer East Route to display the treasures collected and used by the imperial family. There are the Twenty-Five Imperial Seals chosen by Emperor Qianlong for the use of political, military and cultural affairs. Da Yu Taming the Waters, the biggest jade boulder in the Forbidden City is also displayed here. In addition, there are ivory mat, weaponry, jewelry, furnishings as well as gold bells and jade chime as court musical instruments, etc.

The exhibits Stone Drums bear witness to the ancient Chinese civilization. They were found in Yongcheng, Shaanxi and were made around 374 BC to record the learning of crown prince in literature and martial arts and his participation in state affairs.

Jade Boulder of Da Yu Taming Waters

There is a jade boulder in the back room of the Hall of Joyful Longevity. It is named "Da Yu Taming the Waters" with a height of 224 centimeters, width of 96 centimeters and weight of 5,350 kilograms. This jade of Hetian was transported from Xinjiang to Beijing, going through a journey of 4,000 kilometers and exhausted lots of labor, resources and finance. When the jade arrived Beijing, the craftsmen in Ruyi Guan, the Imperial Painting Studio made the design and molded a same-sized model with wax. This wax model together with the jade was moved to Yangzhou, where the craftsmen carved it. It was then moved back to the Forbidden City and placed in the Chamber of Joyful Longevity. It took ten years to complete such a huge project.

"Everlasting Rule" Gold Cup

The luxuriant and elegant "Everlasting Rule" Gold Cup is made of gold and inlaid with precious stones. The Gold Cup originally was wine vessel and then was given the implication of territory and state power. The name of the cup has a meaning of completeness: with no imperfection and no loss would the country be blessed with everlasting rule. On the New Year's day, the Qing Emperor would fill the Gold Cup with Tusu wine and write auspicious wishes as "Eternal Peace under the Sun", "Everlasting Happiness and Longevity" to express good wishes for the new year and the state.

Gold Stupa

The Gold Stupa was the offering in the Buddhist room of the Hall of Respect, where Emperor Qianlong lived as a prince. 85 kilogram gold was used to make it. Inlaid with precious stones and pearls, the top of stupa is decorated with cat's eye and the canopy is adorned with more than 1,000 small pearls. The sides of the top and body of the stupa are inlaid with big pearls, turquoises, corals and other precious stones. It is very colorful, finely patterned and extraordinarily precious.

Gold Bells and Jade Chime

These musical instruments were used to play "Zhong He Shao Yue" (Beautiful Music of Harmony) during grand ceremonies. In the early years of the Republic of China, the small court of Puyi still lived inside the Forbidden City. At the excuse of being hard in keeping balance for the livings of the royal family and his courtiers, he pawned this set of Gold Bells together with some 100 pieces of gold ware, including gold seal, gold album and gold stupa at an extremely low price of 800,000 silver yuan to the Bank of Salt Industry. After the establishment of the People's Republic of China, the Central Government took back the whole set of the Gold Bells from the Bank of Salt Industry in 1953 and put it into the collections of the Palace Museum.

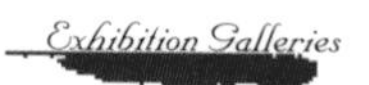

Imperial Parade Armour

This Armour was dressed by Emperor Qianlong during grand parades. Made of 600,000 small steel pieces and connected with gold threads, it weighs 18 kilograms.

The Gallery of Stone Drums

Details

About the origin of stone drums, there are many versions. One version is that they were unearthed near Yongcheng, Shaanxi and date from 310 B.C. to 307 B.C. They describe how the crown prince Yingdang improved his literary level and practiced martial skills. The text was written by Yingdang's teacher and carved by a skilled artisan on ten drum-shaped stones, which were placed in a temple in Yongcheng. Yingdang only reigned four years as King Daowu of the Qin State and left no posterity behind. During the chaotic period after his death, his teacher had the drums buried at Wuzhiyuan near Yongcheng, with the hope that they could be unearthed one day and the facts carved on them could spread to later generations.

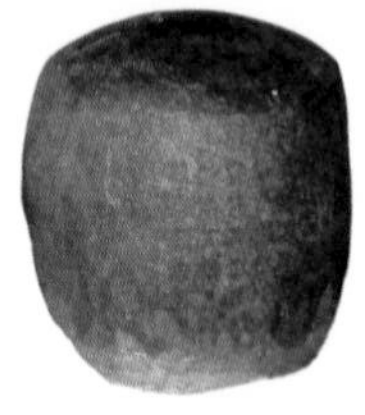

Rubbings

The Gallery of Clocks and Watches

The Gallery of Clocks and Watches is in the Hall of Ancestral Worship. Most of the clocks and watches on display were made in China, Britain and France in the 18th and 19th centuries. The Chinese clocks and watches were made in the Imperial Workshop, in Guangzhou or in Suzhou.

Gilded Copper Musical Clock with The Decoration of Elephant-Drawn Chariot

Most of the British clocks and watches in our collections were made in the 18th century and have different shapes and patterns. This clock is decorated with a group of warriors taking a chariot drawn by an elephant. With springs wound up, the eyes, trunk and tail of the elephant can move and it is the same with the four wheels of the chariot and the wheel under the belly of the elephant. This clock is of great scientific and artistic value.

Gilded Copper Clock with the Decoration of a Writing Figure

This work of art was made by Williamson, a well-known clockmaker in Britain. It is unique in its mechanical driving. With springs wound up, a western figure in suit began to write eight Chinese Characters: "Ba Fang Xiang Hua Jiu Tu Lai Wang" (All coming to pay homage to the emperor). The strokes were done with force and the calligraphy is well composed and very elegant. It is a great surprise that a clock made by a western man could write such beautiful Chinese characters. It is a reflection of the craftsman's wisdom and creativity. It also shows the importance of China in the world in the 18th century.

Black Lacquer Clock with The Design of Congratulating on Longevity

It was made in the Qing court with strong national characteristics and adopted traditional architectural form. It is a desk clock with a two-floor pavilion. The stand of the clock is a long table with colored designs of happiness and longevity in black lacquer. The left side of the clock is a setting of comparing with one another for seniority and the setting on the right is immortals congratulating on longevity. All of them can move when springs are wound up. On the top floor, within each of the three windows, there is a small figure with a chiming bowl. When the clock

The Palace Museum has a large collection of clocks and watches, representing the highest achievement in clock making from the 18th century to 20th century. They witnessed the cultural exchanges between China and the world and are a showcase of extraordinary craftsmanship at home and abroad.

strikes, the windows will open automatically and the three figures jump out at the same time knocking on the chiming bowls to indicate the time. Then, they move back and the windows close. It took 5 years for the clock to be made. It is very elegant and is a representative work of the Qianlong period (1736-1795).

In addition to the works made in China, Britain and France, there are clocks and watches from Italy, America, Switzerland and Japan in the Gallery. With different styles and high-level craftsmanship, they are all precious works of art.

The Gallery of Paintings

The Gallery of Paintings is located in the Hall of Military Glory on the west of the Three Front Halls.

The Palace Museum has 140,000 pieces of paintings in its collection, including famous paintings of renowned painters of various times. The exhibits in the Gallery of Paintings systematically show the development and achievement of the ancient Chinese calligraphy and paintings.

There are works of the earliest well-known painters, Gu Kaizhi's *Nymph of the Luo River* (*Luo Shen Fu Tu*) and *Ladies' Benevolence and Wisdom* (*Lie Nv Ren Zhi Tu*) in the Eastern Jin Dynasty (317-420). Han Huang's *Five Oxen* (*Wu Niu Tu*) is the most reliable authentic work of the Tang dynasty (618-907). Zhang Zeduan' s *Going up the Bian River on Qingming Festival* (*Qing Ming Shang He Tu*) is the most famous long scroll of all times. Li Di's *Hawk and Pheasant* (*Feng Ying Zhi Ji Tu*) is the largest hanging scroll of flower-and-bird paintings in the Song dynasty (960-1279). Wang Ximeng' s *A Thousand Li of Rivers and Mountains* (*Qian Li Jiang Shan Tu*), the Northern Song dynasty (960-1127), is the most splendid blue-and-green landscape painting. Together with other representative works of the grand masters of different schools, these paintings are the essence of the tradition of ancient Chinese paintings. In the collection of calligraphy, there is the earliest masterwork, Lu Ji' s *A Consoling Letter* (*Pingfu Tie*) of the Western Jin dynasty (265-316). Wang Xun' s *To Boyuan* (*Boyuan Tie*) in the Eastern Jin dynasty

Five Oxen

(317-420) is the only authentic work of the Three Rare Treasures of the Qianlong emperor. Feng Chengsu' s *Prologue for the Gathering at Orchid Pavilion* (*Lan Ting Xu*) in the Tang dynasty (618-907) is the copy most close to Wang Xizhi's work. *Eulogy of Launching the Campaign* (*Chu Shi Song*) of the Sui Dynasty (581-618), which disappeared for 60 years and reappeared in 2003, was the most costly calligraphy ever acquired by the Palace Museum. Mi Fu's *Yan Shan Ming* (*Inscriptions on Hill-Shaped Ink Stone*) in the Song dynasty (960-1279) and the *Ten Odes* (*Shi Yong Tu*) as the only authentic work left by Zhang Xian of the Song dynasty (960-1279) are also rare works of art. In the exhibition, you can find many Palace Books printed in the Hall of Military Glory. It is the first time for these books to be shown to the public. You can also find here the history of the Qing court's activity in compiling, collecting and printing books.

Eulogy of Launching the Campaign, cursive calligraphy of the Sui dynasty once disappeared for a long time

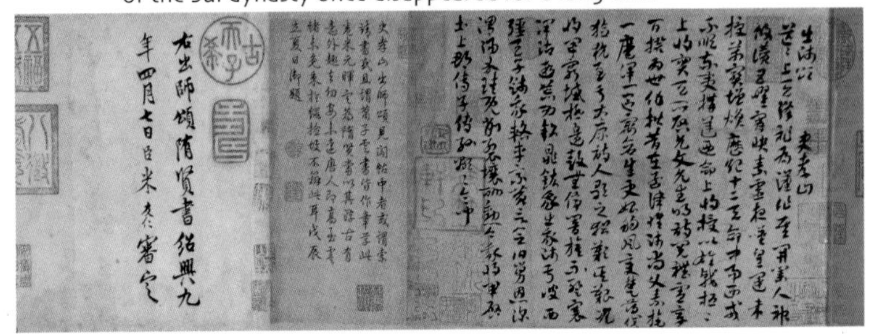

Nymph of the Luo River

To Boyuan

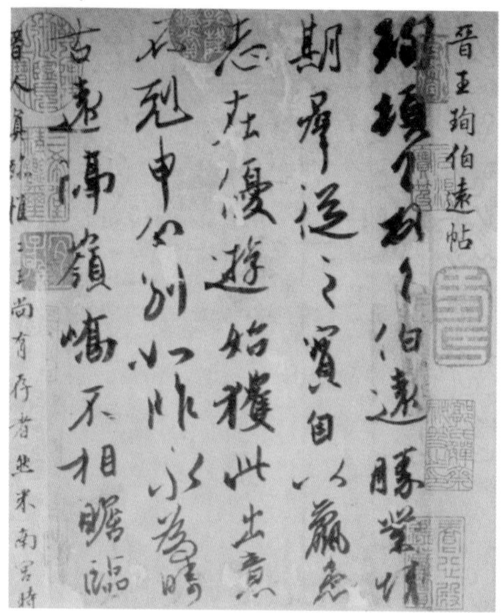

The Gallery of Bronzes

The Gallery of Bronzes is in the Palace of Obeying the Heaven. The origin of Chinese bronzes can date back to 3000 B.C. They are historical witnesses to Chinese culture and oriental civilization. The appearance of bronze has an epoch-making significance in the development of productivity. Bronze was closely connected with politics, economy, philosophy, culture and technology of that time. The Palace Museum has a collection of over 15,000 bronzes and only 148 bronzes are on display.

Nine Elephant *Zun*

Nine Elephant *Zun* was also called You *Zun*, because the inscription on the bronze is the clan emblem You. The shape is round and short with nine elephants and continuous tile patterns. This style and shape are very rare compared with other bronzes. Bronze culture was at the height of its splendor in the Western Zhou dynasty (c. 1100 BC-771 BC). The shape and pattern of this *Zun* are simple but delicate, with inscription skillfully cast and beautifully written. It is a masterwork of the late Western Zhou dynasty.

Relevant Knowledge

The splendid bronze culture created by hard-working slaves is the essence of Chinese artistic history and marks the highest level of craftsmanship in the slave society. It is a very important part of ancient Chinese cultural heritage.

Lotus and Crane *Fang Hu* (Rectangular Jar)

In the Spring and Autumn period (770 BC-476 BC), the Kingdom of Zhou declined and various states prospered. The influence of this change on bronze was the decrease in the number of royal ritual objects. Lotus and Crane *Fang Hu* was a masterwork of that time. Its themes are the animals and plants living in water and on land. It is huge, complicated and elegant. The pattern was novel. The cover is decorated with two layers of openwork lotus petals with a fluttering and singing crane standing in the middle. The crane looks vivid, light and delicate. The body of the bronze is covered with complicated designs of snakes, birds, tigers, flying dragons and coiled dragons.

Bronze *Hu* (Jar) with the Scenes of Banquet, Hunting and Battling

In the Warring States period (475 BC-221 BC), with the development of iron-casting technique bronze became daily objects. This *Hu* is delicate in style and refined in technique. There are 178 figures from the mouth to foot, accurately depicting the living and battling scenes of that time. The content is rich and the figures are vivid. It has great archeological value in the research of social custom, production, life, war and architecture of the Warring States period (475 BC-221 BC).

The Gallery of Ceramics

The Gallery of Ceramics is planned to be moved to the Hall of Literary Brilliance, which is on the east of the Three Front Halls. The ceramics on display dates from the Neolithic age to the Qing dynasty. The Chinese ceramics has a continuous history of 8, 000 years and is a unique wonder in the history of arts and crafts. The exhibits in the Gallery of Ceramics are arranged in chronological order to show the development of ancient ceramics in China.

Cup with Chicken Motif

Underglaze and overglaze colors are unique color painting technique invented in China. Porcelain of the Chenghua period (1465-1487) is noted for its fine body, unctuous glaze and subtlety. The Cup with Chicken Motif is so small and delicate that you can hold it with the part between your thumb and the index finger.

Imitation Porcelain

The development of Chinese porcelain came to its peak in the glorious reigns of Kangxi (1662-1722), Yongzheng (1723-1735) and Qianlong (1736-1795). Famille-rose and enamel colors invented in the late Kangxi period became mature after the development in Yongzheng and Qianlong periods and became the main decoration techniques of overglaze coloring in Jingdezhen. Porcelain imitating animals, plants, rocks, lacquer, wood and bronze is called "Imitation Porcelain". This kind of porcelain is vivid, true to life and as beautiful as original. It fully represents the high level of porcelain production at that time.

The Gallery of Jade

The Gallery of Jade is in the Palace of Cherishing Essence in the East Route.

Chinese Jade has a history of 7,000 years. This gallery is a guide to the general history of ancient Chinese Jade. The collection here includes tools, insignia, ceremonial objects, burial jade, household utensils, stationery, furnishings, ornament, etc.

Jasper *Qi* (Axe)

The works made of Hetian jade in Xinjiang appeared first in the Xia and Shang dynasties. The decorative patterns were mainly presented in double lines and patterns in relief. The Jasper *Qi* was the collection of the Qing court and could date back to Guanghan Culture. It fully represents the artistic style and great achievements of that time and is extraordinarily rare in the world.

Jade Figure of Weng Zhong

Many ornaments named Weng Zhong appeared in the Han Dynasty (206 BC-220 AD). It is said that Weng Zhong was a general in the Qin dynasty (221 BC-206 BC). His surname was Ruan. He was very brave and had won many battles. Everyone who fought against him feared him. Emperor Qin Shihuang ordered to have his bronze statue built before the Xianyang Palace as a memorial and made this statue a symbol against evil spirit. It was in the Han dynasty that the people began to make standing figure of Weng Zhong in jade. There is a hole in the jade for daily wear to get rid of the evil.

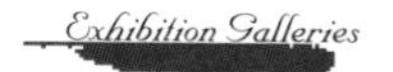

Green Jade Dancing Figure

With the reopening of the Silk Road and the cutting of the Grand Canal in the Sui and Tang dynasties, cultures of the Western Regions (a Han dynasty term for the area west of Yumenguan, including what is now Xinjiang and parts of Central Asia) came to the Central Plains. New patterns of flower, bird and figure influenced by Western Regions and Buddhism appeared for the first time in jade. The Dancing Figure was based on an image of the Western Regions. The other examples are the Jade Flying Apsaras, Jade Lion and Jade Peacock. They were all influenced by Buddhism and the remote culture in the West Regions.

White Jade Cup with The Shape of Lotus Leaf

Jade in the Song (960-1279), Liao (916-1115) and Jin (1115-1234) dynasties were more pleasure-oriented, far less ceremonial-purposed than before. Great advancement was made in the technique of creating openwork at various layers. The jade was mainly dedicated to expressing the people's thoughts and feelings. What the people were concerned was "where there is a design, there is an implication; where there is an implication, there are auspicious wishes." It was a breakthrough to the traditional view of regarding jade as a gentleman' s virtue. Exhibits, like the White Jade Cup with the Shape of Lotus Leaf, White Jade Pendant of Openwork Fish and Lotus and White Jade with Openwork Phoenix Worshiping the Sun all express auspicious wishes for happiness, prosperity and longevity by using synonyms and similar pronunciations of flower, bird and fish.

Jade Falcon Biting Wild Goose

The jade-making techniques in the Yuan dynasty (1271-1368) achieved an unprecedented level in making three-dimensional openwork at many layers to gain perspectives for the design. Variety and forms of jade were adapted to the needs of the public. A lot of works of folk art appeared: Jade Falcon Biting Wild Goose implicates that the small can beat the big; Five Relations symbolizes the feudal ritual system; Autumn Mountain and Spring River show the travel of a Yuan emperor. They are very important in providing material objects for ancient jade research and gaining an understanding of the social history of that time.

The Gallery of Enamel and Cloisonné

The Gallery of Enamel and Cloisonné is in the Palace of Revering *Yang* in the East Route. There are more than 100 enamel and cloisonné works of art on display, which date from the Yuan dynasty (1271-1368) to the Qing dynasty (1644-1911) and reflect the splendid achievement in enamel and cloisonné in ancient China. They also show us the creativity of the Chinese people in absorbing other cultures to develop traditional craftsmanship.

The enamel techniques in China can be divided into two categories: One is cloisonné and the other is panted enamel.

Among the exhibits, there are Cloisonné Burner with Entwined Lotus and Two Ears of the early Ming dynasty, Rectangular Cloisonné Dish with Seven Lions Playing a Ball of the Xuande period (1426-1435), and Painted Enamel Pot with Copper Body and Handle of the Qianlong period (1736-1795). They are all excellent works of art.

The Cloisonné with copper body is very popular in China. It was introduced into China from Arabia at the end of the 13th century. Because the enamel objects were very popular in Jingtai period of the Ming dynasty (1450-1457) and the basic color of the objects was generally blue. It was called Jingtai Lan. Lan means blue in Chinese.

Cloisonné Burner in *Ding* style

Cloisonné Burner in *Ding* Style

The gilded copper body is decorated with cloisonné in rich and bright glazes. The style of the Burner is very typical in the late Yuan and early Ming dynasties with lotus petals as the motif on the neck and foot. This design made the burner more stable and exquisite.

Painted Enamel Pot with Copper Body and Handle

Made by "the imperial workshops of the Hall of Mental Cultivation", this pot was in octagonal shape with a painted enamel and aventurine handle. The patterns of landscape, bird and flower on the pot were all painted by famous painters in the court. The design was avant-garde and artistic. With patterns of traditional Chinese painting in a western-style pot, it is a clever combination of the eastern and western cultures. Different techniques like metal production, enamel firing, glass processing and painting were adopted in one object. It is an excellent work made in the Qianlong period (1736-1795).

The Gallery of Court Operas

The Gallery of Court Operas is located in the Building of Watching Operas and the Tower of Pleasant Sounds, the former imperial opera theater.

The exhibits are from the former collection of the Qing Court, including scripts, stage properties, costumes and headgears. There are also precious photos of the great actors in the late Qing dynasty, such as Chen Delin, Yang Xiaolou and Tan Xinpei. More than 110 exhibits reflect the entertainment activities enjoyed by the Qing emperor and empress, bringing to life the prosperity of

Mei Lanfang in theatrical costume

Script of *Ding Jun Shan*

Court Operas in the Qing dynasty.

It was an indispensable part of court life in the Qing Dynasty to watch operas. Court operas were most popular in the Qianlong (1736-1795) and Guangxu (1875-1908) periods. Whenever there was important festival and grand ceremony, like the birthdays of the emperor and empress, wedding and the New Year's Day, the emperor would call some courtiers to the Forbidden City to watch operas as an expression of imperial favor.

Costume and Stage Properties

The Imperial Household Department took care of costume making for the Court Operas, which was very complicated. The actors were forbidden to bring their own costumes to the Forbidden City except for a few special operas. The costumes were made in the Imperial Textile Bureaus in Hangzhou, Suzhou and Jiangning (Nanjing today) with great variety and high quality, therefore very expensive. Among the costumes and headgears displayed in the west part of the Gallery, there is an official robe with gold designs of dragons, which was an excellent work of the Qianlong period (1736-1795). The designs are rich and harmonious. The colors are splendid and majestic. Finely made by hand, it looks bright and new.

Stage properties

Theatrical Costume

Unopened Areas

Unopened Areas

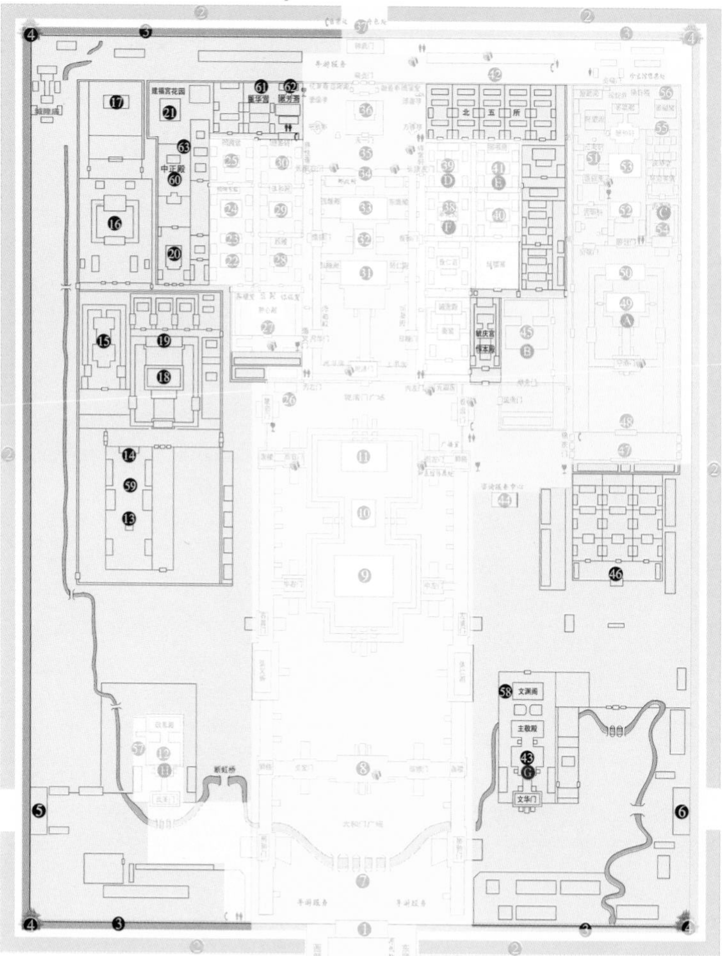

4 Corner Tower

5 The Gate of Western Flower

6 The Gate of Eastern Flower

13 The Garden of Benevolent Tranquility

14 The Tower of Benevolent Protection

15 The Palace of Longevity and Good Health

16 The Palace of Longevity and Peace

17 The Hall of Eminent Flowers

18 The Palace of Benevolent Tranquility

19 The Hall for Worshipping the Great Buddha

20 The Pavilion of Rain of Flowers

21 The Garden of Creating Happines

43 The Hall of Literary Brilliance

46 The Three Southern Courtyards

58 The Pavilion of Literary Profundity

59 The Complex of Benevolent Tranpuility

60 The Hall of Central Uprightness

61 The Palace of Double Glories

62 The Lodge of Fresh Fragrance

63 The Palace of Creating Happiness

There are many reasons why the Palace Museum does not open all areas to the public. Some are already destroyed and unable to open, like the Garden of Creating Happiness, which was used by the Small Court of Puyi after his abdication, but was razed to the ground by a mysterious fire in 1923 and is now under reconstruction, the Imperial Household Department and the Imperial Workshops. Some become offices, like the Place for Editing the Qing History, the Three Southern Courtyards, the Palace of Longevity and Peace and the Hall of Mental Transmission. Some are under restoration or preparation for exhibitions, like the Palace of Benevolent Tranquility, the Hall of Imperial Peace and the Palace of Longevity and Good Health. We are going to give a brief introduction of some important areas to help you know the Palace Museum as a whole.

The Hall of Literary Brilliance

The Hall of Literary Brilliance is on the east of the Hall of Supreme Harmony. It was burned down during the attack of Li Zicheng in Beijing and was not rebuilt till 1682, the 21st year of the Kangxi reign.

The Hall of Literary Brilliance was the residence for crown princes in the Tianshun (1457-1464) and Chenghua (1488-1505) periods of the Ming dynasty .

The Hall of Literary Brilliance, the place where the Ming and Qing emperor discussed Confucian classics and gave tea banquets

The Pavilion of Literary Profundity

The Pavilion of Literary Profundity was the storage for the precious books presented to the Ming emperors as gifts. When Li Zicheng took Beijing, he had the Pavilion burned down. It was not rebuilt till the 39th year of Qianlong' s reign (1774). In the 47th year of Qianlong's reign (1782), the compilation of *Complete Library in Four Divisions* was completed and it was put in storage here. In order to manage and improve the *Complete Library*, several people were selected from the Grand Secretariat and Imperial Academy to do proofreading.

The exterior of the Pavilion of Literary Profundity

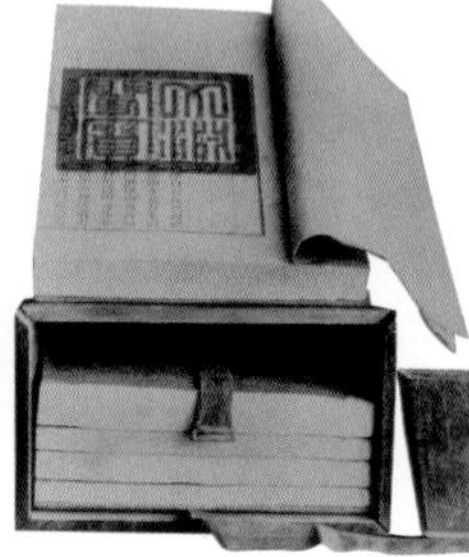

The box storing books in the *Complete Library in Four Divisions*

The book shelves in the Pavilion of Literary Profundity

The Palace of Benevolent Tranquility

After the custom of burying alive with the dead was abolished, the Palace of Benevolent Tranquility was built in the Ming dynasty for the consorts of the previous emperor to live in. Emperor Dowager Xiaozhuang is the first person living here in the Qing dynasty. The Qing emperor would pay respects to the empress dowager here once in the morning and once in the evening. During the festivals, it was here that the emperor dowager accepted the felicitations of the emperor, empress, concubines and officials.

There are a number of halls for worshipping Buddha in the Complex. In the Qing dynasty, a two-storied building was converted into a large hall for worshipping large Buddhist statues of the Past, the Present and the Future. The Garden of Benevolent Tranquility is like a Buddhist world, where 108 Tibetan Buddhist sutras were worshipped; chanting and religious rituals were also held here.

The Lodge of Universal Likeness, also named the Building of Ten Thousand Buddha in the Garden of Benevolent Tranquility

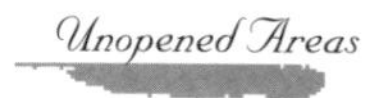

The portrait of Empress Xiaozhuang in informal costume

The Hall of Eminent Flowers

The pipuls in the Hall of Eminent Flowers

The Hall of Eminent Flowers, the hall for worshipping Buddha in the Ming and Qing dynasties, is famous for two pipuls, whose bodhis with golden lines is called "Treasured Bead" and was usually granted by the emperor as special reward. Fond of these pipuls, Emperor Qianlong often wrote poems to praise them, some of which are carved on the stele housed by a pavilion between them. Now, the carved Manchu and Chinese characters on this stele are still fairly clear.

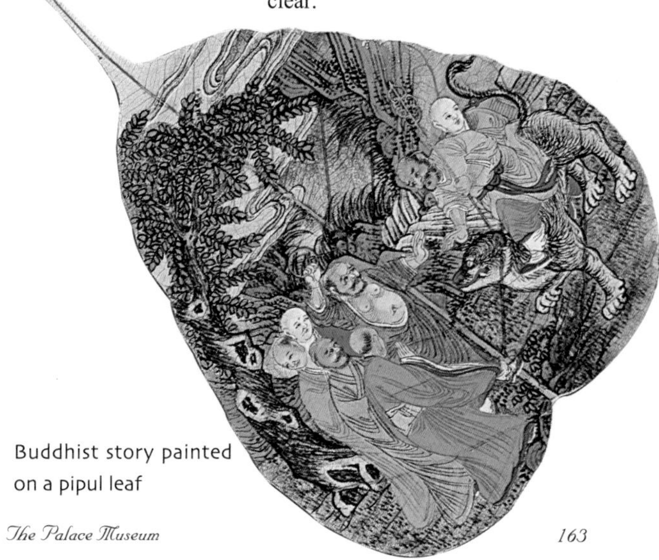

Buddhist story painted on a pipul leaf

The indoor scene of the Hall of Central Uprightness

The Hall of Central Uprightness

North to the Gate of Spring Flower and south to the Garden of Creating Happiness, the Complex of Central Uprightness mainly consists of the Hall of Central Uprightness, the Pavilion of Fragrant Clouds, the Hall of Treasured Flower, the Pavilion of Rain of Flowers and the Tower of Buddhist Origin. In 1923, the buildings northward from the Hall of Treasured Flower were burned down. Now the Garden of Creating Happiness has nearly been reconstructed and the reconstruction of the Hall of Central Uprightness started in 2004. Soon the former glory will reappear, but the original furnishings can only be alive in your imagination. In the Ming dynasty, the Hall of Central Uprightness was an important place to hold Daoist rites. In the Qing dynasty, it became one of the earliest halls for worshipping Buddha and housed a large number of Buddhist statues and paintings from Tibet and Mongolia.

Standing Tara statue made in Qianlong period

The Pavilion of Rain of Flowers

After the style of the ancient Tibetan temple Tholing, the Pavilion of Rain of Flowers was first built in the ninth year of the Qianlong Period (1744). With its copper roof shiny in the sunshine, four unique copper dragons on its roof and Tibetan-styled decorations under its roof, the Pavilion seems to have three floors but actually consists of four floors. It is a typical Tibetan feature that between the outer and inner beams there is a dragon coming outwards.

Its four floors respectively symbolize the four stages of Buddhist practice. In the center of each floor, there is a niche for the red copper Buddhist statues corresponding to each stage of the Tantric practice. In the days for worshipping Buddha, the Qing court would send lamas to chant sutras in different floors. In the side building on the east, the painting of the Living Buddha and national preceptor, Zhangjia the third is worshiped and there is one hanging screen showing the image of Qianlong as the Bodhisattva Manjusri; The painting of the Sixth Panchen Lama, who passed away in the Temple of the West Yellow Sect during his stay in Beijing for congratulating on Qianlong' s birthday in the 45th year of the Qianlong period (1780), is in the side building on the west. The Tower of Buddhist Origin now preserves the firelock and gunpowder container presented to Emperor Qianlong by him.

Detail of Mandala in the Pavilion of Rain of Flowers

The Pavilion of Rain of Flowers, a unique hall for worshipping Tibetan Buddha

The Palace of Double Glories

The Palace of Double Glories is the general name of a palace complex, which mainly consists of three buildings in one courtyard, i.e. the Hall of Respect in front, the Palace of Double Glories in the middle, the Lodge of Emerald Clouds at the back. The Lodge of Fresh Fragrance is located on its east and the Garden of Creating Happiness is on the west. In the Ming dynasty, this area was known as "Five Western Courtyards" and used as the princes' residences. At the age of seventeen, the Qianlong emperor of the Qing dynasty got married here as a prince. After he ascended the throne, his former residence was upgraded according to feudal rules, so it was renamed to the Palace of Double Glories and reformed in a large scale into a luxurious palace with its own style.

The "Fu" (happiness) written by the emperor, given to his officials at the beginning of the spring and regarded as a great honor

The Hall of Respect played the role of sitting room, where there are a throne in the middle for him to accept felicitations and a horizontal board inscribed with the Chamber of Joyful Benevolence written by him when he was granted the title "Treasured Prince" in the spring of the twelfth year of the Yongzheng period (1734). The Palace of Double Glories was his bedroom and its west part was his nuptial chamber. His wife's dowry a pair of nanmu cupboards is still standing against the north wall. Situated at the back, the Lodge of Emerald Clouds served as his study.

Qianlong emperor also initiated verse linking at tea banquet, which became an important cultural activity in the Palace of Double Glories.

@ Links

Linking Verses at the Tea Banquet in the Palace of Double Glories The Qianlong emperor was fascinated with tea. As he enjoyed drinking tea and composing poetry, he held tea banquets in the imperial palace after ancient men of letters and refined scholars. Every spring, the Emperor would invite scholars and members of the Imperial Academy to the Palace of Double Glories for a tea banquet, at which the "Three Purities Tea" named for its freshness and fragrance would be served. It was boiled by snow water with fingered citrons, plum blossoms and pine nuts. All the participants were learned scholars. At the order of the Emperor, their beautiful verses would be transcribed and then hung on the walls of the Palace. From the existing calligraphy on the walls of the Palace of Double Glories, one may get a glimpse of this elegant cultural activity.

Tieluo calligraphy

Writing the Character "Fu" (Happiness) in the Palace of Double Glories When winter began, the Qing emperor would give auspicious characters like "Fu" (happiness) and "Shou" (longevity) written by himself to his consorts, princes and court officials so as to show the generous imperial kindness. This activity started from the beginning of the Qing dynasty and lasted for more than 200 years. After the Palace of Double Glories was built, the Qianlong emperor would come to the Lodge of Fresh Fragrance every year on lunar December 1st to write the first "Fu" (happiness) for the coming spring, which would be hung in the main hall of the Palace of Heavenly Purity.

Small indoor stage named "Feng Ya Cun" (elegance retained) with refined taste

The Lodge of Fresh Fragrance

When the Palace of Double Glories was built, the Lodge of Fresh Fragrance was specially constructed as an entertainment place to show the refinement of the Qianlong emperor. With its shape in "工" and its layout fresh and lively, it has a distinctive style. In its courtyard, there is a large stage for performing operas during imperial festivals. The name of the back hall is "Jin Zhao Yu Cui" (Gold Shiny and Jade Pure), in the east of which there is a horizontal board with the inscription "Gao Yun Qing" (affection with high clouds) written by the Qianlong emperor, and in the west of which is a small indoor stage named "Feng Ya Cun" (elegance retained) set for the imperial family to appreciate the highlights of operas at family banquets.

During the festivals, the emperor would come here to appreciate operas after he had received felicitations. Emperor Dowager Cixi was especially fond of operas. She once ordered famous actors, such as Tan Xinpei, Chen Delin, Yang Xiaolou and Mei Lanfang, to come into the Forbidden City to present performances.

The Garden of Creating Happiness

Constructed in the fifth year of the Qianlong period (1740), the Garden of Creating Happiness is a 4,000-square-meter Garden converted from two of the Five Western Courtyards.

In 1923, the Xun Di (emperor of abdication) Puyi suspected his eunuchs of stealing treasures and planned to check all the storages in the Garden of Creating Happiness. On the night of June 26th, the whole palace was fired. The fierce fire burned down the classic garden constructed at the order of the Qianlong emperor. Later, the cleared-up ruins were converted into an imperial tennis ground.

Now, the Palace Museum is carrying out the reconstruction project of the Garden of Creating Happiness, which has already rebuilt the Pavilion of Extending Spring and some other buildings.

The ruins of the Garden of Creating Happiness

The last Empress Dowager Longyu (the fourth from right) with concubines and maids in the Garden of Creating Happiness

The traces of the Garden of Creating Happiness left behind

The Three Southern Courtyards

As residences for princes in the Ming and Qing dynasties, the Three Southern Courtyards consist of three independent but side-by-side courtyards, the middle one is the Hall of Gathering Fragrance and served as residence of the crown prince. In the Ming dynasty, the Hall was named the Hall of Respecting Origination and Palace of Origination and Root, meaning that the crown prince was the root and origination of the whole country. One of the three famous cases of the Ming dynasty called "hitting case" occurred here. On 4 May of the 43rd year of the Wanli Period (1615), an unknown man with a club in his hand entered the Gate of Eastern Flower and headed towards the residence of Zhu Changluo, the crown prince, attempting to kill him. After the man was arrested and interrogated, the Wanli Emperor felt awkward since the case might have something to do with his favorite concubine, so he hastily wound up this case by labeling this man as "mad" and had him executed.

The Three Southern Courtyards lived by the princes in the Qing dynasty

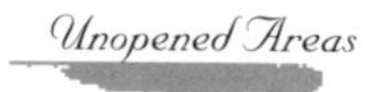

The Hall of Gathering Fragrance

Since the crown prince Yonglian beloved by Emperor Qianlong died young in the Hall of Gathering Fragrance, the Emperor felt very sad with the feeling that the Hall was an unlucky place and decided to reconstruct it completely and placed an altar in the Hall for blessings of safety and peace. Afterwards, the princes would move there only on auspicious days, which should be figured out by the Imperial Astronomical Bureau and then determined by the emperor with red writing brush.

The Imperial Qing family had a complete set of plans and regulations to raise princes up and cultivate them. After the princes were born, they would be separated from their mothers and could only meet them at grand ceremonies. The imperial family placed great emphasis on the welfare of the nation and was afraid that the princes would be enforced obedient by the relatives on their mothers' side. As soon as a prince was born, he would be taken care of by a wet nurse and 40 servants. After he was ablactated, eunuchs would take the place of these people and teach the prince eating, talking, walking and other skills. At the age of six, he would be taught to practice imperial regulations. From he was 12 years old until he got married, he would learn the Chinese language, equitation and archery. After the wedding, if his father was on the throne, he would continue living in the Three Southern Courtyards and if his father had already died, he would live outside the Forbidden City together with his wives and children.

The Important Scenic Spots Near The Palace Museum

The Gate of Heavenly Peace

Known as the Gate of Succeeding the Heaven in the Ming dynasty, the Gate of Heavenly Peace was changed to its current name at the beginning of the Qing dynasty and was the very place for holding national ceremonies and issuing important edicts, e.g. the edict announcing the new emperor ascending the throne. It is towered with a high pavilion and looks very splendid. There are seven white bridges called "Outer Golden Water Bridge" over the imperial river in front of it, two pairs of stone lions on the northern and southern ends of the bridges, and a pair of ornamental columns representing the nation on the left and right sides in the south.

The Gate of Origination, the only pass to the Forbidden City from the south to north

The Gate of Origination

With the same shape as the Gate of Heavenly Peace, the Gate of Origination has a pair of ornamental columns in its south. The east and west low buildings on the sides of the imperial road leading to the Meridian Gate were the offices of the six ministries of the Ming and Qing dynasties. With its side gates respectively leading to the Altar to the Gods of Earth and Grain and Imperial Ancestral Temple, the Gate was the place to store the articles used by the emperor for his hunting, touring and offering sacrifices in the Ming and Qing dynasties.

The plaque inscribed with The Gate of Origination

The Imperial Ancestral Temple

Located on the east of the Forbidden City, Imperial Ancestral Temple was built in the 18th year of the Yongle period in the Ming dynasty (1420) with the function of worshiping ancestors. The emperor would come here on the first day of lunar July, at the end of lunar December as well as in the first month of every season, showing that the most important filial duty should be respecting ancestors. In lunar September of the first year of the Shunzhi Period (1644), Dorgon placed the memorial tablets of Nurgaci and Huangtaiji here in order to show that the Qing had finished the unfulfilled wish of the ancestors in conquering the Central Plains.

Imperial Ancestral Temple of
The Ming and Qing dynasties

The Archway of Defending the Peace in Zhongshan Park

The Altar to the Gods of Earth and Grain

Built in the 19th year of the Yongle period in the Ming dynasty (1421), the Altar to the Gods of Earth and Grain (She Ji Tan) is situated on the west of the Forbidden City, with "She" meaning the god of earth and "Ji" meaning the god of grain. The Altar is an over-one-meter-high three-layered terrace, on which there is the earth in five colors contributed from the whole country, with yellow earth from the center of the country, green from the east, red from the south, white from the west and black from the north, representing the five elements and the lands in five directions. In its center, there is a square stone column named the Stone of Territory Owner or the Stone of State Power, symbolizing that the court would be blessed with an everlasting rule.

The Altar was converted into Zhongshan Park in 1914. Its prayer hall was renamed Zhongshan Hall in memory of Dr. Sun Yatsen (whose another name is Zhongshan), the pioneer of Chinese revolution. To the north of the south gate, there is a white marble archway with blue-glazed tiles, which has witnessed the humiliations suffered by the Chinese people during the invasions of the imperialist countries and the efforts of the Chinese people in striving for freedom and peace. It is the memorial archway erected by the Qing government to commemorate the German Baron von Kettler and originally stood at the crossroads of Dongdan. After World War I ended in 1918, it was moved to the Zhongshan Park and renamed Archway of Insisting on Truth. In 1952, the newly founded People's Republic of China renamed it again to the Archway of Defending the Peace. The new name was written by the famous Chinese scholar Guo Moruo and inscribed on the lintel of the Archway.

Imperial Archives

Located on the east side of the Nanchizi Street, Beijing, it was constructed in the 15th year of the Jiajing period (1536) as the imperial archives to store historical documents and records. The six-meter-thick walls are built with bricks and stones and pierced with stone windows in the north and south, so that the indoor temperature could be stable and air could flow at the same time. Besides, the Archives are armed with furnishings against fire, moisture and insects. With official documents in them, the camphor wood chests wrapped with gilded copper are placed on a one-meter-high white marble stand. With all these well-designed conditions and environment, the imperial documents can be kept for long time.

Imperial Archives for storing historical documents

North Lake

North Lake

Covering about 71 hectares, Bei Hai (North Lake) is one of the most famous scenic spots in Beijing, and is the earliest and most completely preserved imperial garden in China.

The construction of Bei Hai originated from an old legend: it is said that on the vast Eastern Sea stand three celestial hills, i.e. Penglai, Yingzhou and Fangzhang, on which live many immortals who could live forever. According to this legend, the Han emperor had a lake dug in the north of his capital, Chang'an and named it Taiye Lake. He also had three hills piled up on the Lake and named them Penglai, Yingzhou and Fangzhang. From then on, the Chinese emperors enjoyed building imperial gardens after the style of "one lake and three hills".

In the Ming and Qing dynasties, Bei Hai was known as the West Imperial Garden outside the Forbidden City. In August 1925, it became open to the public. In 1961, it was listed as a major historical and cultural site under state protection.

Appendix

The Ming Emperors

Name	Years of Birth & Death	Reign Period	Reign	Temple Title
ZhuYuanzhang	1328-1398	1368-1398	Hongwu	Taizu
ZhuYunwen	1377-?	1399-1402	Jianwen	Gongmindi
Zhu Di	1360-1424	1403-1424	Yongle	Chengzu
Zhu Gaochi	1378-1425	1425	Hongxi	Renzong
Zhu Zhanji	1399-1435	1426-1435	Xuande	Xuanzong
Zhu Qizhen	1427-1464	1436-1449	Zhengtong	Yingzong
		1457-1464	Tianshun	
Zhu Qiyu	1428-1457	1450-1456	Jingtai	
Zhu Jianshen	1447-1487	1465-1487	Chenghua	Xianzong
Zhu Youcheng	1470-1505	1488-1505	Hongzhi	Xiaozong
Zhu Houzhao	1491-1521	1506-1521	Zhengde	Wuzong
Zhu Houcong	1507-1566	1522-1566	Jiajing	Shizong
Zhu Zaihou	1537-1572	1567-1572	Longqing	Muzong
Zhu Yijun	1563-1620	1573-1619	Wanli	Shenzong
Zhu Changluo	1582-1620	1620	Taichang	Guangzong
Zhu Youxiao	1605-1627	1621-1627	Tianqi	Xizong
Zhu Youjian	1610-1644	1628-1644	Chongzhen	Sizong

The Qing Emperors

Name	Years of Birth & Death	Reign Period	Reign	Temple Title
Nurgaci	1559-1626	1616-1626	Tianming	Taizu
Huangtaiji	1592-1643	1627-1636	Tiancong	Taizong
		1636-1643	Chongde	
Fulin	1638-1661	1644-1661	Shunzhi	Shizu
Xuanye	1654-1722	1662-1722	Kangxi	Shengzu
Yinzhen	1678-1735	1723-1735	Yongzheng	Shizong
Hongli	1711-1799	1736-1795	Qianlong	Gaozong
Yongyan	1760-1820	1796-1820	Jiaqing	Renzong
Minning	1782-1850	1821-1850	Daoguang	Xuanzong
Yizhu	1831-1861	1851-1861	Xianfeng	Wenzong
Zaichun	1856-1875	1862-1874	Tongzhi	Muzong
Zaitian	1871-1908	1875-1908	Guangxu	Dezong
Puyi	1906-1967	1909-1911	Xuantong	

Posthumous Title	Numbers of Sons and Daughters	Location & Name of The Tomb
Emperor Gao	26/16	Zhongshan,Nanjing/Xiaoling
Emperor Hui	2	Unknown
Emperor Wen	4/ 5	Tianshoushan,Beijing/Changling
Emperor Zhao	10/7	Tianshoushan,Beijing/Xianling
Emperor Zhang	2/ 2	Tianshoushan,Beijing/Jingling
Emperor Rui	9/ 8	Tianshoushan,Beijing/Yuling
Emperor Jing	1/ 2	Jinshan,Beijing, Jingdiling
Emperor Chun	14/5	Tianshoushanj,Beijing/Maoling
Emperor Jing	2/ 3	Tianshoushan,Beijing/Tailing
Emperor Yi		Tianshoushan,Beijing/Kangling
Emperor Su	8/ 5	Tianshoushan,Beijing/Yongling
Emperor Zhuang	4/ 6	Tianshoushan,Beijing/Zhaoling
Emperor Xian	8/ 10	Tianshoushan,Beijing/Dingling
Emperor Zhen	7/ 9	Tianshoushan,Beijing/Qingling
Emperor Zhe	3/ 2	Tianshoushan,Beijing/Deling
Emperor Min	7/6	Tianshoushan,Beijing/Siling

Posthumous Title	Number of Sons and Daughters	Location & Name of The Tomb
Emperor Wu Emperor Gao	16/ 8	Shenyang/Fuling
Emperor Wen	11/14	Shenyang/Zhaoling
Emperor Zhang	8/ 6	Zunhua, Hebei/Xiaoling
Emperor Ren	35/20	Zunhua, Hebei/Jingling
Emperor Xian	10/ 4	Yixian, Hebei/Tailing
Emperor Chun	17/10	Zunhua, Hebei/Yuling
Emperor Rui	5/ 9	Yixian, Hebei/Changling
Emperor Cheng	9/ 10	Yixian, Hebei/Muling
Emperor Xian	2/ 1	Zunhua, Hebei/Dingling
Emperor Yi		Zunhua, Hebei/Huiling
Emperor Jing		Yixian, Hebei/Chongling
		Hebei/Yihualong
		Imperial Graveyard

图书在版编目（CIP）数据

故宫／故宫博物院编.—北京：紫禁城出版社，
2006.3
ISBN 7-80047-546-8
Ⅰ.故... Ⅱ.故... Ⅲ.故宫－简介－英文
Ⅳ.K928.74
中国版本图书馆CIP数据核字（2005）第128210号

故　宫

故宫博物院编

策　　划：陈连营 张　楠 江　英
中文执笔：罗文华 李　旻
英文翻译：李绍毅 张　彦 杨　帆
责任编辑：江　英
装帧设计：王孔刚
图片提供：林　京 张　楠等
责任印制：马静波

出版发行：紫禁城出版社
（北京景山前街故宫博物院内）
制　　版：北京华艺创世印刷设计有限公司
印　　刷：北京佳信达艺术印刷有限公司
开　　本：889 × 1194　印张 5.75
字　　数：55千字
图　　版：217幅
印　　次：2006年4月第1版第1次印刷
印　　数：1-10000册
书　　号：ISBN7-80047-546-8/J · 250
定　　价：40.00元